THE
MORMON
EXPERIENCE

THE
MORMON
EXPERIENCE

JOLENE & GREG
COE

HARVEST HOUSE PUBLISHERS
Eugene, Oregon 97402

Scripture quotations are from the King James Version of the Bible.

The names of certain persons and places mentioned in this book have been changed in order to protect the privacy of the individuals involved.

THE MORMON EXPERIENCE

Copyright © 1985 by Harvest House Publishers
Eugene, Oregon 97402

Library of Congress Catalog Card Number 85-60128
ISBN 0-89081-486-4

Printed in the United States of America.

To my Lord and Savior Jesus Christ for the furthering of His work upon this earth. To my husband, Greg, and my six children—Justin, Joshua, Benjamin, Brandon, Jennifer, and Michael —for their encouragement in this project, and for graciously allowing me time to write what the Lord has placed on my heart.

As a family we have endured many trials. Now we celebrate the unity we have in Christ Jesus our Lord.

Preface

There was once a rich young man who was very good. He was so good that he could truthfully claim that he had kept all the laws of his church since he was a boy. But when confronted by the Good Master, he was told to sell all that he had, give the proceeds to the poor, and follow the Master in order to obtain eternal life. But because of his pride and self-sufficiency he found the price too high, and he went away sorrowful (Matthew 19:16-22).

It is difficult to convince a moral person of his need to follow the Good Master, Jesus Christ, and it was certainly so in my case. It was impossible for me to consider myself lost and in need of a Savior. Because I was trying to live a righteous life, I could not accept the biblical teaching that there is none righteous, no not one (Romans 3:10).

This is my story—the story of a person delivered from a life of self-righteousness to one whose righteousness is found in the Lord Jesus Christ. It is a story of redemption and reconciliation, in my spiritual life and in my family life.

I write so that you too will be prompted to prove all things, holding fast to that which is good (1 Thessalonians 5:21) and becoming like the Christians in Berea. For it was said of them that they were open-minded and gladly listened to the message. They searched the Scriptures daily to check up on the teachings they had heard to see if they were really so. As a result, many of them believed (Acts 17:11,12).

Jolene Coe
Tempe, Arizona

Contents

— *Chapter 1* —

The Family Of Gods

The preaching of the cross is to them that perish foolishness, but unto us which are saved it is the power of God.

1 Corinthians 1:18

I was proud to be a Mormon. As a young girl still in elementary school, my goals in life were already determined, and the road to achieve those goals was before me. There was no young person in my church as motivated to achieve them as I. Raised in a closed society among Latter-day Saints, all my desires were found within the church, and the life of the church was my life.

Wonderful blessings were promised me if only I would serve the church and my family, and strive for perfection in that duty. My first ambition was to receive the "patriarchal blessing," a foretelling of future events and blessings in my life. Usually given boys and girls when they are 18 or 19, I was asking for mine by the age of nine.

Marrying a young man of the Mormon priesthood in a Mormon temple was my next important step, a step toward godhood. It was imperative that I be linked to a marriage partner in order to be exalted after death and enter the Celestial Kingdom, where we would remain married and would procreate forever. My future, both before death and after, was centered on my family. Being devoted to my husband and bearing his children was my purpose for being. The Mormon way was a family way, and it was *my* way.

Families are forever. It is seen on bumper stickers and needlework, and in magazine and television advertisements. It is a slogan, but it is also a teaching that characterizes a minority of families in America today. Because the family is in jeopardy, the message of this catch phrase has caught the general public off guard.

To our family this was more than a slogan—it was a way of life. We embraced not only the motto but all the teaching that accompanied it. At the heart of this teaching was the importance of establishing close family ties and of doing good works, developing leadership skills, and being an instrument of peace. All of this teaching was for the glory we were to receive in our next life.

However, this did not seem to answer all the questions that kept rising to the surface of my mind, questions that would not go away. These were honest questions to which I was looking for honest answers, and the answers would determine whether I had made the right decision in dedicating my allegiance to my faith.

Where did I come from? What is the purpose of my life on this earth? Where will I be after this life? Is this life real or an illusion? Are the events in my life programmed, or do I have a will free from external constraints? Is my religion a crutch, or is it valid? These and other questions were perplexing, yet important to me during my formative years. It was not good enough to "just believe," as I was told to do many times. Nor was it good enough to accept an answer solely on the basis of the influence of authority, or an opinion held by the majority, or by a process of rationalization, or on the strength of my emotions.

I found myself driven to the pages of my Bible for answers. There I began to see what God teaches about Himself in His Word, rather than relying only on what other people taught about Him. I began to grasp a true picture of God as I looked at His Son, Jesus Christ (John 14:9). As a result, I clearly saw the disparity between my childhood concept of God and what was on the pages before me.

Most people have an inadequate view of God, and to me, God had been a policeman or judge who made me feel guilty or unhappy when I did something wrong. To overcome my unacceptable behavior I believed that I had to give myself to Him in order to gain salvation.

Twelve was an age of discovery for me. It is an age of discovery and transition for most people as they move from childhood into adulthood. Not only are there physical changes, but changes within the emotions and mind. It was during my twelfth year that I began to show my independence by questioning the beliefs of my childhood training. This was not an act of rebellion but an act of making these beliefs my very own. Anything less would have meant that I had been acting on borrowed beliefs.

As I began searching for answers to questions, I knew that they would have to be consistent and noncontradictory with Scripture. And from my study of the Bible, I realized that Jesus would have to be the Lord of my life, no matter what.

Being self-centered and willful, my life was not always a testimony of my beliefs. This caused pain and confusion, but God was gracious and began a new work in me. It has not been without disappointments, but there has been no disappointment in Him. It has been lonely at times, but He has never left me alone. This new relationship with Him has been like a journey, and it began while I was still in my parents' home.

My parents, John and Elizabeth, created a home that

was filled with love and security. It wasn't a perfect home, but it was intact, meaning that both parents were there, and it was a place where we were always welcome. Their home was characterized by unity, a goal toward which we all worked. We worked together and played together, shared our moments of happiness and moments of pain, and found strength in each other. Our family life gave definition to the word "family."

Their three girls and two boys were not mere boarders in their home, but were all valued and nurtured. Rules for living together in the home, along with the sure and quick discipline that followed the breaking of the rules, convinced us of their love for us. This was not a home where everyone did what was right in his own eyes, but a home where we obeyed the rules out of respect and love for one another.

John, my father, had lived with his mother in Phoenix, Arizona, until he joined the Army at the end of World War II at the age of 18. During these formative years, his father was frequently absent for long periods of time, and no one knew where. His mother was supported by her church, the Church of Jesus Christ of Latter-day Saints, and it was from the church that my father received his religious and moral training.

Growing up with a father who chose not to live with his family caused John to experience the harshest form of rejection. And because his father would not provide for his own family, the church welfare department provided. This turned out to be a lifelong source of embarrassment that left indelible impressions.

A transformation occurred in my father's life in 1961 that affected our family life for a number of years. That year his fifth child, a son, was born. Doctors discovered that the baby had an undeveloped liver, and there was no hope given to save his life. After living with us for six months, he passed away. Broken, unable to accept his child's death, and with the belief that the habits of his life caused him to produce a baby that was less than perfect, my father in his grief turned to alcohol. Although his actions were in direct disobedience to the instruction of the Mormon Church, my father continued in his ways while insisting that his children uphold the church doctrine and teaching.

My mother, Elizabeth, was born and raised in Western Michigan. Both of her parents lived out their lives in service to friends and strangers. They would give of themselves and their possessions to help anyone in need. The only daughter in a family with two boys, she was the center of affection in the family, partly due to the special physical care that she required.

She battled against a disease of the lungs. At the age of 15, her condition became intolerant of the cold and wet climate of Michigan, and her parents were forced to move to Arizona for her survival. The disease slowly progressed, and in her thirties the doctors gave her an ultimatum that a lung must be removed to prolong her life.

Following surgery, my mother was close to death. In deep despair my father bargained with God and begged Him to restore her to health. "If she lives, heavenly Father, I will never again touch another drink."

My mother recovered—she won the fight against her lung disease. My father stopped drinking, true to his promise, and became strong where he was once weak. Instead of merely tolerating these difficult circumstances, they took control of their lives and overcame the obstacles. Whatever the struggle, my parents were survivors. This strength they imparted to their children. "Face your problems and don't run from them," they would admonish.

The tough experiences of life that my parents survived helped them develop such admirable qualities as confidence, self-control, pride, and integrity. They always seemed to be able to rise above their problems. Yet these same experiences caused them to not easily admit to any weaknesses, insecurities, or fears. But when we children knew there was conflict and problems at home, these denying, defensive mechanisms resulted in times of emotional distance, reduced communication, and tension that pulled us apart.

One of the memories of my father from my high school days is seeing him in our backyard with his racing pigeons. He was a lover of all of nature, and his fascination and appreciation went far beyond the average person. He derived great pleasure from seeing anything in nature which most of us would overlook, such as watching a bud develop to a flower and then complete the cycle as a mature fruit. His love for nature was imprinted on me, and this love was one of the dearest things we shared in common.

Every afternoon he could be found in the corner of our backyard gently caring for his racing pigeons. He raced these pigeons as a hobby, but we all knew that they were much more than a hobby or just birds to him. They were a source of peace in his life, a relationship free of conflict.

If I wanted to go to the high school football game, my mother would say, "Ask your father." That meant going outside and calling for him. "Daddy, do you think it would be okay for me to go to the game tonight?" For a long while there would be no answer. But I knew that if I stood there and quietly watched the pigeons, he would eventually respond. Finally, in a low and loving tone would come the words, "I don't care." With a bright, "Thank you, Daddy. I love you!" I would return to the house and leave him to his thoughts and his birds.

My father was not only interested in his children when they were old enough to understand and participate in his activities, but he was even interested in us during our early childhood. For hours at a time when I was a baby, he would walk with me in his arms, back and forth across the lawn in the warm air and sunshine behind our house.

During these moments he would hug me close to him and talk softly to me, giving me that feeling of warmth and security. Although this was part of my therapy for a prolonged case of pneumonia, it was definitely an act of love on his part.

Mother found her contentment, security, and peace in providing for the needs of her family. Her greatest joy was found in the unity of her family; she was most happy when we were together.

I remember her at her best during one family outing that nearly ended in tragedy. We had built a cabin in the mountains of Northern Arizona and spent many weekends together there. On a trip to the cabin to celebrate Thanksgiving, our camper truck in which we were riding with all of our supplies for the weekend slid off the road. It was a mountainous gravel road, very slippery with mud, a result of some recent winter storms. Our truck rolled off the shoulder of the road and down an embankment in the darkness of the night.

After we collected our wits and checked to see if there were any injuries (there weren't), we worked together for an hour to get the truck back onto the road. The truck was relatively undamaged so we were able to drive it back onto the road with the help of our family pushing, straining, and hoping.

Once at the cabin, we began to unload our supplies from the camper. Since we were unable to find our flashlights due to the accident, I grabbed a candle and lit it to provide light in the back of the camper. As I put the candle through the door of the camper, it exploded into a huge flame, blowing the camper apart and consuming all of our supplies for the weekend.

Unknown to us, a can of gasoline had spilled in the camper, filling it with vapor when our truck bounced down the embankment.

Instead of considering the weekend ruined, Mother led us in salvaging enough canned goods from the ashes to make a Thanksgiving dinner. She said, "The most important part of Thanksgiving is being together with your loved ones. We have enough food for a meal, and we are not going to let the fire steal our happiness and our Thanksgiving."

Her strength, her positive outlook, and her ability to turn a disaster into a memorable lesson for all of us are characteristics I admire in her.

However, there were times of tension between my mother and me. As in any relationship between parent and child, some of this tension can be caused by the growing independence of the young individual. The time of weaning, the first steps, the first secret, a difference of opinion, the first boyfriend, and eventually the decision to marry can all be points in life that produce tension. This is not a moving against one's parents but a moving toward independence.

Because of my strong will, there may have been a greater amount of tension between my mother and me. Being the middle daughter, I didn't have the responsibilities and freedom of my older sister, and I didn't have the innocence and limitations of my younger sister. Sometimes it was difficult to know just how to fit in.

While my mother and I loved each other, I felt I could not live up to her expectations of perfection. Because she excelled in all her activities, I looked for approval and recognition from her when I excelled in mine. Those special moments when I did receive a compliment satisfied all my insecurities.

Because I did excel in nearly everything I tried, my mother came to expect that kind of performance from me. When I failed at something, big or little, she was devastated, and she chastised me with words about what a terrible daughter I was.

Living as a "survivor" was one of the most valuable lessons my parents taught me. By their words and example, I learned the importance of self-control and leadership. The church teachings also reinforced this approach to my life. We were told as children that we too would need to learn to become survivors.

Self-reliance was the theme behind all the training I received in the church. It was not only important in this life but for the life hereafter. Part of that teaching meant that I was responsible for my salvation and exaltation by doing good works. These good works would show my worthiness, and divine assistance could be obtained only after doing all possible on my own to achieve these goals.

My mother converted to the Church of Jesus Christ of Latter-day Saints at the age of 19, when she and my father were married. My father's family was among those Mormon pioneers who came West to establish Mormon settlements in Utah and Arizona.

The LDS Church taught me many lessons during my formative years, for which I am thankful. It provided many occasions of happiness I now cherish. There were the Daddy-Daughter dates and the Primary Penny Parades (in which we collected pennies for handicapped children in the church's children's hospital). And there were the church-associated camps, church-sponsored achievement programs, and church-affiliated road shows.

The LDS educational program was the most influential force in my life during my preteen and teenage years. From the age of six we were taught church doctrine, first in simplified ways and then in a more complete form as we grew older. We learned the importance of tithing 10 percent of our income, the moral teachings on obedience and chastity, and the Word of Wisdom (which prohibits caffeine, cigarettes, and alcohol). And we were schooled in the 13 Articles of Faith that Joseph Smith gave the church to guide the life of every Mormon. In our church the indoctrination began early, and reinforcement never stopped. The focus of the teaching was to be obedient to the laws and ordinances.

We were taught that our spirituality was based on these

laws and ordinances regarding our conduct. "We believe that through the Atonement of Christ, all mankind may be saved, by obedience to the laws and ordinances of the Gospel," states the third Article of Faith. To live within these laws would guarantee our purity in this life and our salvation hereafter.

In one sense, what I learned about salvation was comforting because everyone will be saved, which meant to us that everyone will be resurrected. However, I also learned that there was more to achieve than heaven: There were levels of heaven. And the levels of heaven I attained were dependent on the degree of salvation I achieved. This was solely dependent on my good works carried out in this life.

The human progression of all this ends in godhood for everyone, with each person eventually having his or her own earth to populate and rule. Jesus stands as an example of a man who did this: He exalted Himself to the position of Christ because of His good works. Being once like each one of us, Jesus revealed what we ourselves can become.

The correctness of our doctrine of salvation and exaltation was reinforced in many ways. I particularly remember how we used to testify to it during "Fast and Testimony" meetings. This was a time when we would all build each other up, giving each other support to keep believing in the church. "I know that the church is true; I know that Joseph Smith is a true prophet of God, that he was inspired to write the Book of Mormon, that the Book of Mormon is true, that the Mormon Church is the only true church." These statements were always repeated but never questioned or examined.

Another part of the monthly "Fast and Testimony" meetings was to give to the poor the money we would normally spend on food. Having thus prepared ourselves, we would individually present ourselves most righteous and acceptable for our neighbors' viewing. As people shared their testimonies, their weaknesses and inadequacies were kept hidden to show that they were becoming a perfect person ready for godhood.

Not only was there a persistent concern to do good deeds to be observed in public, but there was stress that motivated us to perform at home. Even within my family, I felt pressure to be the perfect daughter and sister. We were called to be perfect, and that perfection was to come as a reward for our works. This kept us from enjoying a true closeness, because we all had different levels of personal righteousness. We couldn't experience the acceptance of a parent or a brother when we did something hurtful or silly. We weren't free to acknowledge our very human mistakes. We felt the empty loneliness of having no one to turn to when we failed to perform. How I longed to be accepted by those I loved just for being me!

Instead of recognizing that God's grace enables us to confront our shortcomings and that He accepts us as we are, we continued to live a less-than-abundant life. For support along the path to perfection, my family and I surrounded ourselves with other people who were also striving toward the same goal.

While most of my childhood and teenage activities revolved around my church, I also found time for nearly every opportunity that comes the way of a teenager, including gymnastics, track, and cheerleading. I was often the first-place winner in school and citywide track meets. As an all-around gymnast who competed in the floor exercise, the horse, the uneven parallel bars, and the balance-beam events, I brought home many trophies and blue ribbons. My cheerleading days meant recognition from peers and the excitement of being involved in the high school athletic program.

While these extracurricular activities added much to my high school years, I always wished that my parents would share these events with me. Sure they loved me, but it was their approval I wanted from watching me run in a track meet, or perform in a gymnastic meet, or lead yells with the cheerleaders.

The thought crossed my mind that my parents might be more pleased if somehow I did better in my church activities. But I was already president of my high school Mutual Improvement Association class, vice-president of our school seminary, and president of our Sunday school class. In addition, I sang solos in our sacrament meetings and participated in dance festivals. I had always tried to achieve a higher position in the church because it was the way to attain a higher position in heaven. And because of the eternal consequences, great expectations were put on me by my parents and church. What more could I do?

Just as the Israelites were commanded to teach their children the laws, so it was in our home. Our regular topic of conversation was our faith—Mormonism and its ideals. Nevertheless, my efforts to be the best Mormon possible seemed to go unnoticed by my family.

As I proceeded through each year of high school, the quiet side of my life increased. Previously, I had been involved in athletics and student government, but now it was reading books, writing poetry, and just thinking. I was thinking about the most basic issues of life—instead of accepting them at face value, trying to understand them for myself. And since I lived in a Mormon world, I began to think about my beliefs, which can be a dangerous thing to do. Yet I had a promise from Jesus Christ: "If ye continue in my word, then are ye my disciples indeed; and ye shall know the truth, and the truth shall make you free" (John 8:31,32).

— Chapter 2 —

Mixed Blessings

Behold, I stand at the door and knock; if any man hear
my voice and open the door, I will come in to him and
will sup with him, and he with me.

Revelation 3:20

For 12 years I lived within the circle of belief of the
Church of Jesus Christ of Latter-day Saints. I was proud
to be a Mormon, and my religion was always the important part of my life as I busied myself with church
activities and surrounded myself with friends from
church. This closed circle of church friends, however, was
suddenly breached by an outsider who had recently moved
into the neighborhood a few doors from mine. Her name
was Cheryl. And because I am incurably social, I was the
first to meet her.

As our friendship began to develop soon after Cheryl
moved in, she invited me to attend an ice cream social
followed with a sermon by the pastor of her church. Never
having attended another church (it was not usually
permissible in my family to attend a church different from
our own), I found the offer both exciting and harmless.

I asked my mother and was surprised when she gave me permission to go with Cheryl and her family. Perhaps she did not know what would take place that night; maybe she pictured it as a family outing rather than an activity sponsored by a church. My mother and I didn't realize at the time that her momentary decision would have far-reaching results. But it is just like God to use the small and seemingly unimportant things of this life for His purposes.

As the pastor introduced his message that evening, I sat quietly, observing everything that took place in the room, anxious to hear what other people learned in their churches. The topic was familiar: salvation. But suddenly I was hearing ideas that were new to me, words that were familiar but used in an unfamiliar way. Because good teaching always evokes questions, many questions formed in my mind. And excitement grew within me, for as the pastor continued, each question was answered as soon as it popped into my head.

"If you're like me," the pastor began, "you've experienced times when you don't feel very lovable, times when you don't feel that you're acceptable by your own standards or by anyone else's, times when you feel as if you're failing at everything you try and disappointing everyone you care about. These times can be very lonely, and that loneliness builds in you a sense of inadequacy and isolation. 'Will anyone ever accept me just for being me? Or will I always have to worry about losing friends when I let them down? Won't anyone accept me as I am?'

"The answer I have for you tonight is, 'Yes, there is Someone who will accept you unconditionally. This Someone also promises forgiveness of sins and eternal life. This Someone is God, our Father in heaven, and all He asks of you is your love for Him and your acceptance of His Son, Jesus Christ. Jesus came to earth as a sacrifice for your sins and for my sins. When we believe this wonderful news, we are welcomed into God's family.' "

The pastor's words of love, salvation, and forgiveness of sins seemed to be directed to my questions and my needs. As he closed his message he said, "Remember John 3:16. Really listen to these words: 'For God so loved the world that he gave his only begotten Son, that whosoever believeth in him should not perish, but have everlasting life.' "

I did listen to those words, and I did long to know this God of love presented as a personal friend. This was all new to me because God had always been taught to me as a big god to whom one should not get personal because it would not show respect for Him.

When the pastor invited the people to come forward and kneel at the altar to pray, I was the first person there to confess my sins and to experience the new birth. The message of God's acceptance and salvation had drawn me to the front of the church, and now I couldn't wait to experience the salvation that Jesus Christ provided.

It didn't seem to take much courage to get up from my seat and walk to the altar at the front of the church in view of everyone because I wanted what the pastor talked about. When I reached the altar, a kindly, elderly gentleman greeted me and asked to pray with me. By my side were Cheryl and her family, also praying. Then the elderly man read to me an appropriate portion of Scripture which opened my eyes to God's saving grace. He explained that the gospel or good news was complete in Jesus Christ, not in anything I could do. It was all accomplished on the Cross. Then he read:

> For the preaching of the cross is to them that perish foolishness; but unto us which are saved it is the power of God. For it is written, I will destroy the wisdom of the wise, and will bring to nothing the understanding of the prudent (1 Corinthians 1:18,19).

When we finished praying and talking at the altar, we were all crying tears of joy. I had met Jesus Christ and now had the assurance that He accepted me! I had come to know the freeing and wonderful love which He offers everyone. However, it wasn't until I was 20 that this decision fully impacted my life.

I was excited and wanted to share this news with my family. I wanted to explain what the unconditional love of Jesus Christ meant.

When we left the church, the car couldn't go fast enough to get me to my house. All the way home I watched the speedometer, once in a while urging Cheryl's father to drive just a little faster. There was important news to share with my family. My heart was pounding with excitement as I said thank you and ran up the walkway and into the house.

It was later than I realized when I walked in the door, and Mother was the only one waiting up. When I saw her there, I threw myself into her arms and began telling her what had happened, of my newfound love for Jesus, and of my desire to live for Him.

This was the first time that we had ever had a deep and personal conversation about God. Being a private person, my mother would never discuss serious matters with me, whether it was about our beliefs or my sex education. She had always thought that what I needed to know about God would be explained in Sunday school, and that a discussion of God would be either out of the question or on a superficial level.

So with all my natural enthusiasm I continued to tell her of the wonderful heavenly Father I had. I wanted to explain to her God's forgiveness—His salvation and grace as it was explained to me. In my eagerness to tell her of my experience, I probably put her on the defensive, and her reaction was not what I had expected. She became angry and told me to be quiet. No longer in her arms, I tried desperately to understand what was happening.

And now it was my turn to listen to her.

"This, Jolene, is the very reason why you have not been allowed to attend other people's churches. You have let your emotions overpower your mind. You have let those people distort ideas which you know are right. You were foolish to have fallen into this trap. I do not want you to say anything about this to anyone—especially your sisters, your brother, or your father! And I forbid you to attend any other church. I forbid you to talk to Cheryl ever again! Now go to bed!" I knew better than to cross my mother. Dejected, I walked to my room.

As I crawled under the covers, tears cascaded down my face and I began to weep convulsively because my happiness was not shared by the one I loved most. How could this be, since we Mormons loved Jesus more than other people did? How could anyone reject Him?

I became perplexed about my beliefs and realized that I had never put them on trial to see if they were true. What if they weren't right? What if the Church of Jesus Christ of Latter-day Saints isn't the only way? I had never really considered it. Mormonism was "the truth," a statement we all testified to without examining. Now, however, the things I had heard at Cheryl's church made me wonder how secure the foundations of my faith really were. Why hadn't the pastor mentioned proving my worthiness by good deeds to attain godhood? It was my insecurities about attaining godhood that gave me motivation for some of my activities.

Understanding the doctrines of the church had never been important until now. Instead, everyone from Joseph Smith to my bishop and Sunday school teachers had stressed the "burning in the bosom." This inner feeling was a confirmation of the correctness of the Mormon doctrine.

I remember attending many "Fast and Testimony" meetings where members of the church thanked the heavenly Father for their ability to believe without asking any questions. In my work with the women's Relief Society, I saw this theme reinforced as women were praised for being born with a "knowledge of truth," which made it unnecessary for them to have proof of their beliefs. Although it is important for a Mormon to be knowledgeable, asking too many doctrinal questions was looked down upon. Now, however, the pastor's words had given me reason to question what was once unquestionable.

Being the independent, think-for-yourself type of individual, I did not want to mentally drop out when it came to a matter as important as belief. It was not good enough for me to just believe without proof. Repeating that something was the truth would not satisfy my question. Testimonies of happiness, smiling faces, and positive attitudes were not necessarily proof of correctness of belief, because people from other churches evidenced those same characteristics. Even new converts to the Unification Church, est, meditation groups, and organizations that offer a sense of community and an identity often exhibit these signs.

That night at Cheryl's church the subject of sin was part of the message. Immediately there was a conflict between what I believed about sin and what the pastor explained. I had believed that we came into the world as spotless babies who only later would make mistakes, and that my life would have "rough edges" which would need to be smoothed out. This did not, however, identify me as a sinner, as the Bible stated. But the pastor quoted, "All have sinned, and come short of the glory of God" (Romans 3:23). If I am not a sinner, there is no need for me to be saved and no need for a Savior. There is no reason for Jesus to have died on the cross for me.

This subject of the place of Jesus Christ as the Savior of my life came up again in a request I made of my mother. Once when I had been at Cheryl's house, I noticed that she was wearing a cross and I asked her why.

She explained that without the cross we cannot have salvation. Without Christ's death and resurrection, there would be no hope for our own resurrection. This brought new meaning to the cross for me. Suddenly it was important, a symbol of me accepting Jesus Christ.

This prompted me to approach my mother and request permission to buy a cross. When I asked her she said, "Absolutely not! You will never wear a cross around your neck, so never mention it again! The cross is a disrespectful way to look at Jesus. He is not to be looked at as dead, hanging from a cross, but to be looked at as alive. We frown on this. You don't see Mormons wearing crosses."

To her, it was like asking if I could wear a bloody rabbit's foot around my neck. It made her sick that I would even think of it. She explained that the cross is morbid, that it showed the piercing of Christ's skin and other violent things.

The emphasis in my training had been that we Mormons do not want to remember the cross of Jesus and that His resurrection from the dead is more important. The cross reveals the horrible truth that Jesus was marred beyond recognition and that He suffered death because of our sins. The resurrection, though, stands as evidence of the godhood He supposedly attained, the godhood that each Mormon believes he or she can also attain.

What the pastor at Cheryl's church said also made me wonder about confessing my sins. His message of God's unconditional love and His forgiveness for all my sins made me study another doctrine that I had held since childhood. It was taught in the church that a bishop or stake president needed to be the mediator between God and me, and that there were different degrees of sin and different means of atoning for them.

Although I was only 12 years old, the message I heard was a message I was ready for. When I responded to it by confessing my sins to the true Mediator, Jesus Christ, in prayer at that altar, I knew I was different. There was an inner peace for which I had been searching for a long time.

However, because of my age I had to continue to conform to my parents' teachings. "Forget what happened. Do not return to that church, and don't associate with Cheryl," mother had said. So in obedience I became quiet about my experience.

Unable to nurture the seeds of belief and new life by being with Cheryl and attending her church, I cherished the memory of that evening and the words of the pastor. Being 12, I was a child who did not have a choice in the matter of my religious education and training. But the news of God's love and life in Him had been planted as seeds, and these seeds would mature later when I had the freedom to cultivate them.

In some small way my spiritual life was cultivated during those years that I remained at home, although not in a very visible way. I remember Cheryl's mother saying to me over and over as we drove home from the church that night, "Jolene, you must stay in the Word; you've got to read the Bible on a daily basis." And I did. That began a habit that has continued to this day. Cheryl also would provide encouragement and guidance for my spiritual life as we would have a chance to meet once in a while.

My introduction to God's love and His plan for salvation had happened outside my familiar world. When I returned home, I returned to a strong, exclusive culture that included family and friends, along with goals and a lifestyle that gave me my identity.

I remained a Mormon girl striving to earn acceptance by achieving perfection in all that I did. The same year that I accepted Jesus Christ as my Savior, I worked hard to receive the Mormon honor of my "patriarchal blessing," a highly regarded step usually reserved for people in their teens or early twenties. Because of the tightly knit Mormon culture, it was unavoidable to return to my life as it was before receiving Christ despite the reality of my experience.

I had looked forward to obtaining this blessing ever since I had first learned about it in my primary class at the age of nine. The teacher had explained that this blessing would be something to treasure, that it was a gift from God in which He foretold the future, that it gives a person a plan and a goal for life, that it warns us about the pitfalls which await us as we work toward that goal, and that it would be valid as long as we lived the gospel teachings.

While my girlfriends were more interested in school and boys than in the serious things of the church, I decided that I was ready to receive my blessing.

The first step was an interview with the bishop of my ward in his home. This was required prior to having an appointment with a patriarch. After determining that I was morally clean, Bishop Sorensen asked about my tithing and my attendance record at church activities, and whether I was mature enough to handle the blessing about to be given. His questioning, however, didn't end at this standard stopping point.

"Jolene, you know that you are very young. Your ability to understand is limited. I want to warn you that you may not understand some of the things you will hear. It might be better for you to wait. Furthermore, the patriarch could have a more complete picture of your life if you wait a few years. This is a very significant step, and I want you to be sure that you understand what you are doing."

At times our family vacillated in their commitment to and participation in the activities of the church. But during the times of distance from the church, I continued to be interested in spiritual things. Always listening closely in church and in my Sunday school classes, I was fascinated with discussions about our religion and spiritual things. Now I had the chance to take an important step in my own spiritual life, and I didn't want to wait. The bishop would not discourage me now.

"Bishop Sorensen, I don't want to wait. My age doesn't matter, and waiting a few more years shouldn't matter either. I came to you for my patriarchal blessing, and I want it." Impressed more by my enthusiasm than my reasoning, the bishop said simply, "Okay, Jolene. I see that you are eager to obtain your blessing, and I will arrange it."

For my appointment I went to the patriarch's house, which was a little house near the temple in Mesa, Arizona. It was a very humble setting, a room decorated with white walls and mint green trim and containing just a few pieces of furniture. It gave the impression more of a parlor than a living room.

When I entered the house I was greeted by a very elderly gentleman with white hair, maybe 90 years old. He was the patriarch who would give me my blessing. As he continued his greeting, he motioned for me to sit down on the couch opposite him. As he began questioning me as to whether I was morally and spiritually fit for his blessing, I realized that the same questions my bishop asked me would be repeated.

When the patriarch determined that I was acceptable for the blessing, he led me to a small rectangular room that served as a library. There I was instructed to sit on a certain chair that was surrounded by tall bookcases. He proceeded to walk behind me and put his hands upon my head like a crown.

I strained to hear and tried to remember each of the patriarch's words of instruction. "Sister Jolene," he began solemnly, "I lay my hands upon your head and confer your patriarchal blessing.... If you obey your parents, your children will honor and obey you when you become a mother in Israel....

"Your mission on this earth has many phases. One of great importance is to seek out a man of God as a

companion and husband, one who is worthy of the Holy
Priesthood and the blessings of a temple marriage....
There will be about you throughout your life many noble
men and women who know not salvation or how it may
be attained. You have found the way and the light, and
you may point the way of eternal life to others....

"Live according to the Word of Wisdom and avoid
the sinful practices of society so prevalent in the
world.... Remember the Lord in your tithes and offerings. Obedience to this law will open the windows of
heaven to you.... Even some of your close friends and
associates will tell you it is not necessary or important
to keep the whole law. This is the doctrine of the devil....

"This is your blessing. It is for you to so order your
life for the great exaltation that awaits you. Now, dear
sister, be true to your covenants.... Know that there will
be within you that strength of God to carry you safely
through the trials, troubles, and temptations of life....
I seal this blessing upon you depending upon your faith-
fulness."

I was proud to hear those words. I felt very spiritual.
I had done the proper Mormon thing, and I had done
it at an earlier age than most people. When it was over,
I stood up and thanked him for the blessing. He shook
my hand and said that he felt that my life was a very
important life, that I needed to be strong to the vows,
and that I needed the church. He continued that he had
many more things to say about my life but that there was
something restraining him—he couldn't tell me more.

It troubled me that he couldn't tell me all of what he
knew. I was not afraid of the truth. Even if it would hurt
me, I would rather have known it then. But I didn't
express any of these misgivings to him, but responded
by saying that what he said is whatever I am to have. Then
I left. It was a simple experience that took only an hour
of time, but it was a sacred moment.

— *Chapter 3* —

Reconcilable Differences

Therefore shall a man leave his father and his mother, and shall cleave unto his wife, and they shall be one flesh.
Genesis 2:24

It is not necessarily a law of the universe, but the experience of life suggests that opposites attract. Greg was everything I had always dreamed of. He was not opposite in the sense of always opposing or being incompatible, but in the sense of contrasting. Dark-haired and olive-skinned, he had the suave look and demeanor of a young movie actor. Clean-cut, with carefully groomed hair and nice clothes, he stood out when everyone else was wearing long hair and had adopted the sloppy look. He was always nicely dressed.

Greg was not from a wealthy family, but his parents provided him with many material advantages that would make life advantageous for a teenager. For example, he was about the first person in his high school class to own a car.

By his appearance, you would think Greg was a Mormon, but his ideas and conversation betrayed that thought. He was honest, open, and sincere. Many of the boys from my church were proud, loud, and always dreaming up adolescent attention-getting stunts. They were somewhat immature and unsure of themselves.

Those things were not important to Greg. He was not showy, always calling attention to himself. While my Mormon boyfriends wanted to always be "having fun," Greg would rather go for a walk and have a good conversation. We had great conversations over a wide range of topics from the deeply serious to the personal or even lighthearted. We were not afraid to explore any subject. He was even open to talk about his feelings, something most men find difficult. He exuded a self-assured and confident behavior. He knew where he was going in life and what he wanted to be.

Whatever good or bad came into Greg's life, he would say that it would all be used for God to make him the kind of person He would want him to be. From time to time I thought he wasn't going to make it in life because he didn't know how to do anything on his own—he relied too much on God. This was my rationalization because I had little if any reliance on God. My faith was totally in myself to excel in life, and if I didn't excel the fault would be mine.

Intelligent, patient, and kind, he had many characteristics that a girl wanted in a fellow, and best of all he was available. But Greg was not a Mormon.

As a sophomore in 1971, I could only admire Greg from a distance. Greg was a senior, three years older than I, and his crowd of friends wasn't a part of my crowd. I saw him regularly, but never enough, as we changed classes during the school day. And often those times meant a warm smile, a friendly wave, or an occasional wink. Most of the time, though, I was surrounded by my Mormon friends. I didn't know anybody but Mormons. Besides, I was somewhat afraid of him because I was in the church and he was outside the church. I literally feared that I wouldn't know how to relate or talk to him.

I was proud to be a member of the Church of Jesus Christ of Latter-day Saints. I was pleased to belong to such an elect organization. We felt that we knew the right way to live and that we were taking steps toward godhood as we lived on this earth. We were secure in our beliefs, in our community of church friends, and in our church activities. During the ninth grade I had served as the vice-president of the seminary class of two schools, a significant post for a woman when young men hold most of those leadership positions. And now I had moved on to the presidency of my class in the Young Woman's Mutual Improvement Society, an organization for girls 12 to 17 that provided doctrinal instruction. Free time, such as it was, was filled with the many activities at the ward.

I also felt that I was well on my way to reaching three goals which were extremely important to me. First, I planned to marry a young man who had already completed a mission for the church. This husband would be a devoted Mormon who had spent two years sharing the Mormon gospel with people who did not yet believe it.

Following his faithful service to the church, we would be married, and our marriage would be sealed in the temple. This meant that our marriage would be for time and eternity. No other ceremony would do. It was required of us to be sealed for eternity because, like every other person on this planet, we are gods-in-embryo. We are put on this earth and given physical bodies in order to have the opportunity to prove ourselves worthy of godhood. The Mormon doctrine of eternal marriage teaches that this godhood will not and cannot be attained unless one is in partnership with a spouse, and that this partnership is legitimate only if it has been sealed in a Mormon temple for all eternity. My very godhood was dependent on my achieving this second goal.

Upon marriage, my husband and I would begin a

family. Not only did I personally desire many children, but it was my primary duty. It was the teaching of the church that countless spirits in their preexistent state could only come to this earth if there were earthly bodies for them to inhabit. Without these bodies, the spirits would not be able to progress toward godhood. As a woman, it was my spiritual obligation to provide bodies which would house these spirits and give these preexistent spirits the opportunity to advance.

Compromising my dedication to these three goals of husband, marriage ceremony, and family was the deep friendship and love I developed for Greg.

Greg was kind and well-liked, and it was public to the kids at school that Greg was a Christian. His life displayed a dedication to Jesus Christ for all to see. Needless to say, Greg and his circle of friends were not popular with mine. Because my life was so directed, there was little chance of getting together, yet I hoped that somehow we would have the chance to meet and maybe even date. At the same time this hope ran counter to those goals which I valued and which people expected me to attain. Nevertheless, this hope persisted.

Relationships have a direction to their development, and so it was in our case—from the outside in. It was first Greg's appearance, then his character, and then our compatibility that won my heart. Soon the primary attraction became Greg's relationship to Jesus Christ, and I wanted for my life more of what he had.

In Greg I saw a reality and an authenticity to his commitment to Jesus. His spiritual life was integrated into everything he did. It was a natural part of him, and he wasn't afraid to talk about it. He wasn't afraid to pray or to examine his beliefs, something new to me because these things were absolutely forbidden among people of my church.

The Mormon boys wouldn't think of praying on a date with a girl, but not Greg. If the opportunity presented itself, he was eager to. This was not caused by fanaticism on his part, but because Greg wanted Jesus to be Lord and Master over every area of his life.

My sophomore year at high school quickly ended in summer. This would put distance between Greg and myself, for soon he would be attending college while I remained in high school, and we would each be occupied in our different worlds of church activities. Our paths would go in different directions and would probably not cross again.

On the first day of my junior year I happened to walk past the place in the school where I had usually seen Greg. There was still the huddle of boys that always congregated there. Though Greg was not there, I realized that I hadn't forgotten him.

A sign that summer is over and the school year has begun is the first football game of the season. The 1972 season opened with my school, Westwood, going against Mesa High, our crosstown rival. When Westwood and Mesa High played, everyone turned out. This was the most important game of the season to the city's sports fans and to the students. It was a fun night, and this night was no exception—fresh and crisp, with the dark blue sky punctured by bright stars and the field lights of the stadium.

Four girlfriends and I had arrived early and were successful in taking possession of seats on the 50-yard line. Each girl had worked and primped to be as beautiful as she could. Hours had been spent combing hair in fancy, attractive styles. We all wore new clothes and were walking advertisements for Jordache and Calvin Klein. We had "confidence."

As the players ran onto the field, the crowd was on its feet cheering. The bands were playing Sousa marches and movie theme songs, and the fans were roaring. When I stood to see what was happening down below, one person in the crowd caught my eye. It was Greg! I couldn't

believe that it was him. As I stared at him, I imagined
how it might be if someone introduced us. Maybe we
could go out to a restaurant after the game. Maybe we
could sit together at next week's game. Maybe we could
share our dreams. My fantasy was interrupted when one
of my friends grabbed my arm and pulled me down into
my seat. I had been the only one standing!

As the game progressed, the five fellows who were
sitting a few rows below kept turning toward us and away
from the football action. Once when Greg looked back,
I saw that familiar welcome-wink that had brightened so
many school days the year before. Typical of high school
romances, that series of smiles, waves, and winks developed a special feeling between us. Far from being a
stranger, Greg was already the person I wanted to share
my life with—even though we had never gotten past
"Hi." Needless to say, I was thrilled when we girls were
invited to join the fellows. That was when the unexpected,
but much-hoped-for, introduction to Greg happened.

After the game, this party of five girls and five fellows
paired up and went out for pie. While at the restaurant,
Greg's class ring became a topic of conversation. Jok-
ingly I asked if I could try it on. Once it was on my hand,
the banter continued. "Now that I have it on, I might
as well wear it." Laughter followed, but so did Greg's
refusal when I tried to give it back to him. "No, Jolene,
I really want you to keep it. Will you go steady with me?"
Another wild dream come true—and high school romance
at its best.

That evening marked the beginning of a special association. Our casual acknowledgments of each other the year
before had developed quite naturally into a comfortable
friendship that was richer than most teenage romances.
This richness was because Greg brought Jesus Christ into
our relationship.

Greg talked openly about Jesus, and what he shared
was new to me. I had grown up in the shelter of a church

and had no more than a superficial knowledge of the Bible and what Christianity was about. Because the Mormon Church acknowledges that the Bible is less than reliable, the focus of my training had been based on the words of my teachers and bishops. These words had more to do with trying to live a moral and good life than on knowing God.

Greg often quoted from the Bible, sharing verses that spoke directly and personally to my life. The way he trusted in the Bible and the way he used it were new to me, for we believed that the Bible was God's Word but that we could be misinformed or misled by it because it had been corrupted.

We had many discussions about our churches and their doctrines and ways of life. We carefully explained our beliefs to each other, and both of us seemed astonished at the different ideas we heard. Greg's Baptist training had kept him as protected from my church as my Mormon upbringing had kept me from Jesus and Christianity. Still, he listened patiently and encouraged me to come to know the Jesus he knew. When, for instance, I faced a decision or a problem, Greg asked, "Have you prayed to the Lord about it, Jolene?"

As our friendship grew, so did our love and our sense of being committed to each other. This commitment brought our religious differences into even sharper focus. How could I commit myself to someone who did not believe as I did? The only way it would work for us was to somehow convert Greg to the gospel of the LDS Church. Although I was quite unsure how to do this, I was sure of his feelings for me. Because he loved me, he would change and accept Mormonism.

It wasn't until Greg confronted me one day with a very strange question that I realized he wasn't accepting what I had been telling him. "Jolene," he began, "do you believe in a personal relationship with Jesus Christ?"

"Sure," was my reply. After all, the name of my church

was the Church of Jesus Christ of Latter-day Saints. Actually, I had no idea what Greg meant. The pastor at Cheryl's church hadn't used this phrase, and it wasn't used in the teachings of my church. I thought that this was Greg's way of asking whether my church recognized Jesus.

"Jolene, when were you born again?"

I was stunned. "What?"

"When were you born again?"

At this point, the conversation stopped. I was stalling for time to determine what Greg meant. Like many people, I thought that "born again" was a catch phrase or religious jargon. Little did I know that Jesus used it when He told Nicodemus, "Except a man be born again, he cannot see the kingdom of God" (John 3:3).

Our debate about Mormonism and Christianity continued. Even while defending my faith, I loved Jesus Christ, and my love was sincere. "Don't worry so much about the label. Whether I'm called a Mormon, a Catholic, or a Buddhist, I will be seeking out Jesus. I want to know Him better. Besides, if I am following the wrong Jesus, I will realize it. Until then, Greg, I can't just adopt your faith and your words; it must be my own. I need to know for myself if something is right or wrong. That's the only way I'll be able to live according to a set of beliefs."

Greg accepted my position, always careful not to assault or destroy what I believed in, but he knew I would leave the LDS Church if and when I could no longer accept its doctrine.

Instead, he taught me what it meant to live as a follower of Jesus Christ.

The weeks went by, and we continued to spend more time together attending football and basketball games, going to the movies with friends, and taking long drives in Greg's car. On those drives up to the mountains to view the beautiful Arizona desert valley, we would frequently discuss our different heritages. This was often followed by a drive down Scottsdale's lovers' lane.

As we shared these times, it became difficult to talk freely about our religious beliefs because of the frustration and tears they produced. So we avoided the subject altogether, which was not a method of problem-solving I wanted to bring into a marriage.

While we stopped talking about Mormonism for a while, Greg's parents began discussing it. Aware of the seriousness of our relationship, they felt compelled to learn something, and learn it quickly, about this strange religion. Greg also began to study Mormonism, reading the documents of the church as well as what those "outside" the church had written.

While we had agreed to not discuss our religions, Greg's example kept speaking to me. I envied his ability to cope with difficult situations and wondered about his way of staying calm and hopeful in tough circumstances. Trying to figure him out, I thought that his little expressions of faith in Jesus were just a way of avoiding reality, and that he wouldn't amount to much if he didn't learn to fight his battles for himself.

While I was the one who had been taught not to run but to face my problems and be self-reliant and independent, it was Greg who was best able to cope with life's problems. This he did by trusting in the direction he found in God's Word and by accepting His invitation to bring his problems to the Lord in prayer.

Greg also helped build me up in the faith. "Jolene, you were born again when you were 12. You need to study the Word and learn more about Jesus. You won't have to worry about your salvation—it is assured. And you won't have to worry about us, either. Jolene, the Lord is in our relationship. And when the Lord is directing, we can't fail."

While Greg's words were in my ears, there was a war of emotions raging in my heart. Repeatedly I reminded myself that as a Mormon I had everything. There was my loving family, my many friends, and all the material things I needed. I was a member of the only true church on this earth, and I liked being a Mormon. But intuitively and emotionally I sensed that something was missing.

As Greg and I were planning for a short engagement and then the wedding, we reached a point where we realized that either I would have to give up the LDS Church or Greg would have to be converted in order for us to proceed.

We were both counseled by our parents to terminate our relationship. Both sets of parents advised us that our religious differences would cause conflict, grief, and sorrow in the years to come. It seemed unlikely, however, that either of us would convert. I was frightened by the thought of leaving the familiar world of Mormons and the security of my well-defined role. Outside of my brief friendship with Cheryl, I didn't know any Christians. I didn't know any way to live except what I had experienced and been taught.

Understated, my parents wanted me to remain a Mormon and expected obedience in that desire. They, like all parents in the church, expected their children to hold church positions, to faithfully attend the church meetings, and to tithe. And we were taught that if we obeyed our parents and fulfilled their wishes, our children would obey us when we became older. This principle of obedience, a doctrine of the Church of Jesus Christ of Latter-day Saints, made it hard for me to consider leaving the church. It made me feel guilty—as though I didn't love them even though I knew I did.

My parents charged me with letting God down, of throwing away everything I had been taught, and of making my own bed in hell. Mother would ask, "How can you give up a temple marriage? How can you face the fact that you will not have your children throughout all eternity? How can you face your friends, knowing you have given up everything?''

The strain sapped all energy and ambition from me. Depressed for days, I didn't want to get dressed and go outside. Up to this time I had loved life so much and had savored every day and opportunity. Now I felt that life was being ripped from me.

Likewise, Greg could not consider leaving behind his faith in Jesus. He had begun to study the Mormon Church, its history, and its teachings, and he was not at all open to joining.

Complicating this difficult situation was the fact that Greg already considered me a Christian. ''Jolene, you have been saved by your belief in Jesus Christ. You're just on the wrong path, and you can't help that because you've never been taught how to live for Jesus. You have never had the chance to learn the gospel of Jesus Christ. You need to become grounded in the Word of God; you need to know the Bible and how God wants you to live.''

Greg worked hard to build in me the foundation that I lacked. He wanted me to learn the Bible so that it would become the fabric of my life. The central theme of the Bible is that God sent His Son, Jesus, into the world to save us from our sins. And that theme was the center of our studies.

Still greatly influenced by my parents at the age of 16, I bowed to their wishes and broke my relationship with Greg.

— *Chapter 4* —

Irreconcilable Differences

Be not unequally yoked together with unbelievers; for what fellowship hath righteousness with unrighteousness? And what communion hath light with darkness?

2 Corinthians 6:14

Parents should know better. When they are dealing with their teenagers, they should suggest the opposite of what they really want them to do—at least some of the time. To tell a young couple in love that they should break up is in most cases the wrong thing to say. It's almost instinctive with young lovers that when there is an external threat to their love and relationship, they try all the harder to protect it. And so it was in our case.

We did break up—for a whole month. But Greg and I loved each other so much that we couldn't resist talking and seeing each other several times throughout that month.

Against everyone's wishes, we proceeded with our marriage plans. Greg did not believe there was any reason to break up; he wasn't marrying a nonbeliever. He simply planned to lead his new wife in building a foundation for their life together in Christ.

Our wedding day arrived in February 1973. And in spite of the opposition to the marriage from both sets of parents, we had a very nice, big wedding and reception. My desire was to follow all the traditional wedding customs, and my mother made that desire come true with all her arrangements.

Like most young couples, we were idealistic and didn't realize that after the wedding comes the marriage. We thought we had only married each other. But now we were becoming aware that we had married different ways of thinking, different values, different traditions, and different families. Within six months we found that we had created a situation that was tearing us apart.

The four parents were distraught because of the step we had taken, yet at first they tried to contribute to our marriage in a positive way. Although they meant well, each began offering advice. Sometimes, however, the advice concealed a veiled criticism. Each had their own ideas as to how we should build our marriage. Each had their own agenda.

Not knowing how to deal with these outside forces and lacking the confidence to respond to our parents produced tension between Greg and me that became stifling. Fear of our parents' judgments prevented us from being ourselves and showing our convictions and desires. Instead of joining together to answer our parents, Greg and I moved into separate corners.

I had become absorbed in trying to please my parents to restore my relationship with them, and at the same time my guilty conscience was seasoning my marriage in ways that I found distasteful. They were disappointed and grief-stricken by my turning away from the teachings of the church and throwing away the many blessings which the heavenly Father has waiting for those who are true to the Mormon gospel. I wanted to make things right with my parents, but I didn't know how to.

Repeatedly I discussed this struggle with Greg. I would

begin by telling him that the teachings and community of the LDS Church were important to me. I wanted him to understand that I had tried so hard to stay true to those teachings while growing up.

Usually he listened without much comment, but one night after listening to me for several minutes, Greg took the offensive, grabbed hold of my hands, and made me look straight into his eyes. He wasn't mad but just tired of the whole thing. He had tried everything he knew to help me see what I was getting into, and that I was blind.

"Jolene, Mormonism is a cult. There are no two ways about it. The evidence is there. They have always placed total importance on the church's teachings and commandments. If the Mormon Church were indeed the only true church on the face of the earth as it claims, then why is there no teaching of the cross and the need to repent? That Christ shed His blood for the sins of mankind? Why don't they preach that everyone must be born again, saved, redeemed by Christ alone? Why does the church instead rely on its own teachings and commandments, even though they have changed them so many times over the years, rather than relying on only the Bible? Why do they rely on their Scriptures when there are so many conflicting statements in them? How can that be believable?"

As Greg kept talking, my eyes filled with tears. He continued in a loving, sincere way, always careful not to disparage my beliefs. "Jolene, I am only asking that you give God a chance to work in your life. I know you've been taught to be true to the teachings of your church. But I fear for you because of all the turmoil it's causing in your life and my life, and all I'm asking is that you stay true to the Word of God.

"Think back to when you were 12 and you first heard about Jesus. Remember that evening, Jolene? Remember your joy at discovering Jesus' love for you and the forgiveness of your sins? Remember the freedom you experienced then? He wants you to feel that love and joy and freedom every day. And He gives those things to whoever will follow Him.''

My heart sank. I wanted to believe what Greg was saying to me, but I could not accept the idea that the Mormon Church was a cult. Cult was not a word used in my circle; to me it was a four-letter word. A cult, I had been taught, was a group who worshiped Satan openly, and I neither did that nor ever wanted to be a part of that.

This really turned me off. Up to this point in our marriage we had never fought and were always sensitive about the words we used with each other. So I knew he meant what he said, and that I should take him seriously. While I was still defending my beliefs, I was beginning to consider what Greg was saying. How could I change overnight? The LDS Church had been my whole life, always protecting and guiding me. Besides, people in cults worshiped Satan, and I certainly hadn't been doing that. I had tried to be a good person and live a pure life, and I truly did want God to work in my life. How could my church really be standing in the way of that?

That night I meant business and I opened my mind and heart to carefully listen to Greg as he answered my questions. I wanted to understand both sides and make a decision. I didn't want to continue resisting the truth as it concerned my faith.

Although I didn't understand everything Greg said, things began to make sense. While I understood what he read from the Bible, there was still a part of me that did not want to accept it. I had devoted myself to the Mormon Church all my life, and the thought of leaving it frightened me. My days had revolved around its teaching and program, and my life had been filled with its people. I was thankful to be part of a people whose integrity meant a lot to them, a group whose family and heritage was revered. Leaving the church seemed like betraying a best friend who had always stood with me.

Although opening the door of communication with Greg was an important step, I still felt a tremendous obligation to the Mormon Church and still desired to attend the services for my parents' sake as well as my own needs. As I left home for my church each Sunday morning, Greg headed in the other direction to his.

Although we were discontented with the practice of attending separate churches, we were patient with each other, at least until our first child was born. Following the birth of our first son, at the end of 1973, I realized in a new way the importance of attending church as a family. I begged Greg to attend my church, but with loving and steady determination Greg stood strong. He would not go to the Mormon Church.

Because of this standoff, even further distance was put between Greg and my parents. Rather than sulking or hiding their extreme displeasure, my parents became vocal. They warned me again and again that I was sacrificing my godhood by being married to Greg and that I was forfeiting the great heavenly rewards that await people who are married in the temple. And our son, their first grandchild, would not be with them in heaven unless I was married in the temple; he would be wandering around heaven without a family.

Pulled in different directions by my love for Greg, a desire to please my parents, and confusion about what to believe, I sought the counsel of my stake president. Each session I approached with great hope. But each left me feeling more confused and emptier than before. At one point the president declared that if I loved Greg enough, he would inevitably join the church. But as the days passed, I realized that this was not to be. The possibility of Greg joining the LDS Church was not predicated on my love for him. Greg would not be persuaded by that.

During these months a dark cloud of depression hung

over our marriage. We didn't laugh much, and tears seemed to be a regular part of each day. Avoiding friends and family was my way of coping with the stresses of life. Not wanting to be crushed by the questions and judgments of others, I wouldn't leave the house or answer the phone for days at a time. It was too painful to report the difficulties of trying to solidify my marriage.

These people were well-meaning as they listened and offered their opinions, advice, and "perfect solutions," but their words suggested that they only cared about the church and its requirements. Occasionally I would think that maybe they were insecure as to their own belief and were rousing guilt in me for openly questioning it.

None of them seemed concerned about my commitment to my marriage or about the destiny of my soul. No one other than Greg ever discussed my relationship to Christ or the importance of the marriage vows I had made.

Recognizing the high doctrinal view which the LDS Church places upon temple marriage, it was not surprising that my Mormon friends and family did not acknowledge the sanctity of the vows which Greg and I had exchanged. Church doctrine states that a marriage performed outside a Mormon temple is legitimate only in the eyes of the people and the law; it is not legitimate in the eyes of God. Furthermore, only with a temple marriage could a Mormon girl eventually enter the celestial kingdom, attain godhood, and reign over an earth. That ceremony seals the bride to her husband for all of time and eternity, and she is given a secret name by which he will call her to heaven after they die.

Children also have something to gain from a temple marriage. The temple marriage insures that the couple's children will be sealed to them, without which the children would be lost and left to wander around in the afterlife, unable to enjoy heavenly rewards.

My extended family and friends held firmly to these doctrines. Consequently, they did not view the possible end of my marriage to Greg as a crisis. They only considered that if I stayed with Greg my final destiny would be in a lower kingdom, unable to enjoy the presence of God and unable to progress toward godhood. According to them, I had nothing to lose and everything to gain by leaving my non-Mormon husband.

These days were filled with anguish and despair. Even with this upheaval in my mind and in my family about Mormonism and Christianity, I continued to love Greg deeply. And that love made me ask even harder questions about my church, the most perplexing of which was, How could a church I loved so much advise me to leave my wonderful husband, my beautiful home, and my new-found Christian friends? Repeatedly my Mormon friends presented seductive arguments to "walk away," to "leave while I could," and to "start over while I was young."

When love is threatened it always responds. So whenever I was presented with one of these statements, I remembered that it was Greg's character and spiritual maturity that drew me to him. It was his consistent walk with Christ, his ability in troubled times to rest in Christ and find peace in His promises, and his convictions that confirmed that I had made the right decision.

The opposing forces of my parents and their family, and that of my marriage, were fracturing my life. I began to feel as if two different people lived inside me. First there was a young wife who loved her husband and wanted to be with him and their child. I desired nothing more than the peace and contentment of being with them. My joy was found in serving them, whether it was by changing diapers, cleaning house, or preparing meals.

Second, there was the person whose ambitiousness was rooted in the teachings of her church. I believed I was placed on earth to do more than eat, drink, and be merry. Time and talents were not to be wasted so that I could become anything, even a goddess, if I did certain things in this life. My ambition was to live as a saint in the Church of Jesus Christ of Latter-day Saints, marry in a temple, and be that goddess.

At this time my parents and sisters were extremely disappointed that I no longer was striving for those heavenly rewards. My anxiety and guilt from my family was compounded with a feeling of worthlessness. Because I wasn't involved in the activities of the church, I was not receiving their praise and notice. In the LDS Church one is praised for everything he does, great or small, and I felt worthless because this affirmation had ceased.

Being an extremely ambitious person, there was still a drive within me to be noticed for my accomplishments and to be important. That drive was so strong that at times I was willing to give up my family in search of a Mormon man who would help me reach my godhood.

Six months after the arrival of our first child, I became pregnant with our second. It was the end of summer in 1974, and the physical stress of having a baby combined with the strain of my marital situation confined me to my bed for a month.

I felt trapped and was trapped. The two strong desires inside me were waging a furious war, with only an occasional rest between skirmishes. I began to admit that Mormonism and Christianity were two very different and very incompatible belief systems. Previously I had told myself that the differences were only minor and that they could be surmounted or overlooked—that I couldn't walk away from that which had been my life.

During this time Greg continued to assure me that everything would be fine. He would say, "Jolene, I know the love you have for Jesus Christ is real. You're different from other Mormons. You're not blinded by the teachings of the Church. You really are committed to Jesus Christ." However, he knew that I was headstrong and needed to discover for myself that truth is not found in the church that Joseph Smith founded but in Jesus Christ. He respected me and gave me the freedom to scrutinize for myself.

I was paralyzed by the amount of advice I was receiving. And with each bit of advice came a measure of guilt—some for me and some for the adviser. This is because with each suggestion or criticism offered, a corresponding feeling of guilt is raised in the critic. Everyone wants to justify himself by criticizing others.

My family was sending me messages that seemed to say that time was running out and that if I were going to move back into the Mormon fold it had to be now.

I remember receiving a telephone call from my younger sister. The warm, sunny day was perfect for the landscaping project that Greg and I were working on together, but the summer day's warmth turned to a chill with Ellen's call. "Jolene"—the sound of her voice was a tipoff that she had been crying—"I am grossly ashamed of you. I can't believe that you aren't strong enough to be a member of the church. What is wrong with you, anyway? What is going on? Why have you stopped defending the Mormon Church the way you used to?"

Punctuated by sobs, Ellen's questions were fired off at such a rate that I was unable to respond. Stunned and hurt, I was never given a chance to reply. When she hung up, my own sobbing began. For hours after her call, I lay on my bed with feelings of guilt and rejection. And as I brooded about the conversation in my mind, I became angry at being told I was weak. I felt anything but weak!

Now seven months pregnant, I again decided to visit the stake president for his guidance. This was more out of habit than actually wanting his guidance. Confused, I wanted some answers, but at the same time I didn't want "his" answers. I knew that he would say, "Well, since it isn't going to work out, you better divorce him."

As I drove up to the large brick home with its carefully groomed yard and tall trees swaying gently in the breeze, I thought of the new life within me. What would my

child's future be? Would this child know its father?
Would she be able to climb into her daddy's lap? Would
he be able to play football with his dad? Tears ran down
my cheeks as I considered these questions. The peaceful
setting of the president's home stood in sad contrast to
my inner turmoil. Would I ever have a place to call
"home"? Would this child inside me ever know a happy
family? The possibility seemed slight. I got out of my car
and slowly walked up the long sidewalk, defeated.

That defeat was more of a surrender. I left the meeting
with the stake president's words ringing loudly in my ears.
"Remember, Jolene," he said, "the most important event
in this life is a temple marriage. Without it, you cannot
live with your heavenly Father in the Celestial Kingdom.
It would therefore be better for you to divorce Greg, live
alone, and look forward to being a servant in heaven.
If you stay with Greg, you will perish in outer darkness
because of his beliefs and practices."

This was the darkest day of my life, for I gave in to
the president's advice. The pressure from the Mormon
culture, which includes a network of family and friends,
a belief system, and a way of life, pulled me back in. I
didn't want to divorce Greg because I loved him. The
thought left me cold and empty, and I sobbed for hours
as I struggled for a different solution.

Greg was as committed to being a follower of Jesus
as I was to the LDS Church. The strength of my conviction was in a commitment made years before that I would
die for the church. And that seemed to be coming true.
In choosing the church over Greg, a part of me was truly
dying.

To leave Greg and admit defeat by dissolving our
marriage would take more strength than was in me. I
knew I didn't have the strength to take this step. Then
I remembered my patriarchal blessing and the promise
that my heavenly Father would give me supernatural
power to do what I needed to do.

Desperate, I got down on my knees and asked for strength to get through this difficult time. From somewhere came the power to act on my decision to leave Greg. As I stood up, I felt a firm resolve to get the divorce and to live the way I wanted to live—the way my parents had taught me to live. In retrospect, I believe the source of that power and resolve was Satan, the destroyer. But at the time I didn't understand that.

I continued through the mundane events of the day numb. Suitcase packed, I waited on the livingroom couch with 15-month-old Justin for Greg to return home from work. As soon as he entered through the doorway, he stopped when his eyes fell on us. We appeared to him as though we were going to flee. His eyes filled with tears, his head dropped, and he began to sob.

Instead of sobbing with him as I felt like doing, suddenly I was filled with strength to continue with my plan. Now nothing could stop me. With an unsteady voice, I said, "Greg, I want a divorce. If you don't drive me to my parents' home right now, I'll walk."

Sobbing uncontrollably now and without an argument, Greg put the suitcase in the back of our small truck. He climbed into the driver's seat, all the while holding our son close to him. Slowly he drove the five miles to my parents' house. "You'll be back, Jolene. I know you'll be back. I know that the love you have for Jesus Christ is real...."

Our divorce became final three months later.

— *Chapter 5* —

In My Father's House

That no man is justified by the law in the sight of God is evident, for the just shall live by faith.

Galatians 3:11

It didn't take long for me to get settled into my parents' home, a very large and beautiful house in a peaceful country setting. A freshly painted white rail fence surrounded the manicured front lawn. At one side of the property stood a flourishing orchard which produced every kind of fruit imaginable, and in the back were the horse stables and a large swimming pool. Inside the house, my mother was soon busy baking breads, pies, and cakes to nourish a daughter she had always thought to be a little too thin. These welcome aromas added a homey touch to the well-kept and orderly house, itself a refreshing change from the inner turmoil I had been battling for so long.

Justin and I shared a large bedroom at the end of a long hallway. Each morning bright sunlight filled the room with its warmth, and I spent many uninterrupted hours talking, playing, and just being there with my little boy. Greg's companionship was missed very much, and in some way that need was filled by Justin.

The days at my parents' house also meant time with family and friends, as well as a return to church activities. My old friends welcomed me back as though nothing had happened, and my activities provided opportunity to make many new friends.

Most of our Sundays were spent at church, and week-days were filled with other church-related functions. My schedule was packed with church commitments, and my parents were thrilled when I started to teach the primary class. This new responsibility added more activity to my already busy days. I spent many hours making visual aids, writing lessons, preparing music, and becoming ac-quainted with the children in my class.

Like every Mormon woman, I was also involved in the Relief Society, where we were taught lessons on doctrine, culture (how to interact with society), instruction on the role of a good wife and mother, and home economics. For three hours every week, women of the church came together to learn about chastity and purity, cooking and sewing, and how to be a good wife and mother. They learned about different countries and the women's role in those faraway places. Stories of model women who obey their husbands and accounts of pioneer women who washed clothes, milked cows, slaughtered animals, and started fires—all for their husbands—were shared.

The ultimate purpose of the Relief Society is to strengthen the family, which is the basic unit in the Mormon Church. And it succeeds with a twofold empha-sis: First, the church's doctrine is taught that a woman, being in a lower state, must be linked to a man in the priesthood by temple marriage if she is to reign in the Celestial Kingdom, and second, that she is to concentrate on meeting the needs of her husband and family by her domestic skills. One enters the Kingdom as part of a family rather than as an individual.

My Relief Society met every Wednesday morning, and I looked forward to every meeting, for it was almost a support group for me. Although it wasn't a place to disclose personal problems, eventually the women learned the reasons for my divorce, and they showed sympathy and understanding. They provided me with an abundance of love and friendship that I needed as a newly divorced person and single parent in a world of intact families.

The hectic pace of commitments, meetings, and classes kept me so occupied that I didn't have time to reflect on my past or future. It permitted me to block everything out. In obedience to the church teachings of heavenly rewards from good works performed during this life, I immersed myself in all the activities and requirements of the church. For every member, this entails attending all church meetings, paying full tithe to the church, upholding the Word of Wisdom, supporting the church leaders, believing their pronouncements as doctrine, following the codes of behavior, and marrying in the temple to attain godhood. Only with such earthly conduct is one eligible to be a god. Only with such a sparkling performance record can one possibly hope to reach the Celestial Kingdom.

We had been challenged in our Sunday school class to read the Mormon Scriptures, so I began with the Doctrine and Covenants, followed by the Book of Mormon and the Pearl of Great Price. As a high school freshman I had read the Book of Mormon and enjoyed it, not so much for the content or meaning but for its style—the wording is similar to the King James Version of the Bible. Many times, however, I wouldn't understand what I read, but Sunday school instructors had a standard answer for this situation. Whenever one does not understand a passage he is to pray earnestly, and if he is sincere and if the heavenly Father feels he is ready to learn, He will open his mind and give him understanding.

Acting on this teaching, I spent many hours in prayer,

following the prescribed format of "Dear heavenly Father" and using "thees" and "thous." Even with this "correct" prayer, I didn't understand any more than before. Instead, I seemed to reach the point where it didn't matter whether or not I understood, but that it was simply a great privilege to read the Book of Mormon and the other Scriptures. Understanding what was written was not an important issue. This attitude or mind-set was typical of nearly everyone I knew at church.

Most of my reading was in the Doctrine and Covenants. The Doctrine and Covenants was written in what was an attempt at an Elizabethan style of English. It is wide-ranging in content, from how to live a moral life to presenting most of the doctrines, ordinances, and sacraments of the church.

At the time I was not looking for problems in the text but trying to get rid of my own problems. Yet as I continued to read the Bible along with the Doctrine and Covenants, many disparities, conflicts, and inconsistencies between the two books became apparent.

Yes, I was busy—busy with the Mormon commitments, the Mormon activities, and the Mormon roles which would earn me godhood. Despite this constant busyness, I had an unquenchable longing to read about Jesus and learn more about Him. And the home of my Mormon parents provided me the perfect opportunity for the kind of study I wanted to do. Even the Bible lessons that Greg had shared with me several years earlier would break through that busyness and minister to me.

In my room at the end of the hall were the privacy and quietness that I needed to sort out my thoughts and feelings. With Justin playing beside me, I was able to think through the painful past and consider what the future might hold. My mother allowed me this freedom. She respected my privacy and let me stay in my room for hours at a time. She was sensitive to the fact that it had been hard for me to leave Greg, but at the same time I believe she respected me for taking that step. She also realized that I was an adult and didn't need her to mother me. Also, she had her own busy schedule of activities.

Enjoying the sanctuary of my room, I chose not to go out of the house much. Instead, I spent time in this peaceful setting which could aid in my healing and restoration. In the silence of my room, the pressures from people and what I was to believe were quieted. I secretly reminisced about the precious Savior who loved me so much that He left His home in heaven to live among men and ultimately be crucified on my behalf.

During these quiet moments, the only Teacher I had was the Holy Spirit. With His guidance, I read the Bible carefully, and I began to see more clearly the startling differences between the teachings of my church and the Bible. I realized that there was an ultimate conflict between Mormonism and Christianity and that both could not be correct. Either the Book of Mormon or the Bible was right. I could not follow both, but had to make a choice.

Many questions were forcing me to find answers. Was the Bible the true Word of God? Or was it merely an ancient narrative written by mystics 2000 years ago? What explained its survival through the years? What could account for its historical accuracy and its unity, considering that there were many authors over a span of 2000 years? How could generations of people have trusted that book if it were false?

On the other hand, what proof was there to establish that the Book of Mormon was "the most correct book"? Was it, rather than the Bible, actually the Word of God? Or were the claims of Joseph Smith nothing more than his own imaginings? Had he really borrowed Masonic-like rituals and then chosen certain biblical passages only to make his story come to life?

Was it all to bring himself praise, glory, and wealth? Had he been helped by some supernatural force while he wrote this book? Was this book really the means of salvation that everyone should be following? And what did the church mean by saying that the Bible is reliable "as far as it is translated correctly"?

Still another issue gnawed at me. Why hadn't anyone else discussed the contradictions between the Bible and the Book of Mormon, between Christianity and Mormonism? I had heard none of the arguments and seen none of the evidence against the Mormon Scriptures, doctrines, and history that Joseph Smith professed. While not an expert on these things, I was able to clearly see that these two religions completely contradicted each other. They were not, as I had been taught, compatible and complementary.

At this point I remembered a verse that Greg had discussed with me: "Faith cometh by hearing, and hearing by the word of God" (Romans 10:17). As my faith in Jesus Christ was developing through the reading of His Word, important and difficult questions about my life-long beliefs were also developing.

* Was Jesus a man exalted to godhood because of His good works? This Mormon teaching claims that Jesus' father had earned godhood by his works, as had his father before him and his father before him, on through eternity.

* Was Lucifer (Satan) just one other son of God? Wasn't he one who had failed his father and been expelled from heaven for his disobedience? What else would have led him to set up his kingdom and war against God?

* According to Mormon teachings, salvation is available to all mankind. But isn't the Celestial Kingdom available only to Mormons, and then only if they had been good enough, if they had kept all the church's commandments, and if their marriage has been sealed in the temple?

As I methodically studied the Bible, I kept careful notes. God's Word spoke clearly and directly to my questions about God, Satan, and salvation.

* I saw to my astonishment that the Bible teaches one

and only one God. Deuteronomy 6:4; Isaiah 43:10-12; Mark 12:29; and John 1:1 echo Isaiah 44:6: "Thus saith the Lord, the King of Israel, and his Redeemer, the Lord of hosts: I am the first and I am the last, and besides me there is no God."

* The Bible also explains that Satan is a fallen angel who had been glorified in heaven. He later forfeited his position of high honor when he tried to make himself equal with God (Isaiah 14:12-14 and Ezekiel 28:14,15). For the first time I saw Satan depicted as a figure of pride and selfish ambition who now exists as the deceiver and the tempter of believers (Matthew 4:1; 2 Corinthians 11:14; 1 John 4:1-3).

* Finally, salvation was presented in completely different terms in the Bible from what I had been taught in the Mormon Church. Romans 3:28 was a radical idea to me: "A man is justified by faith without the deeds of the law." This idea is repeated throughout the New Testament (John 3:16; John 14:6; Acts 2:21; 4:12; 16:31; Romans 10:13; 2 Timothy 3:15). What was the true means of salvation? Again, the Bible was specific: "If thou shalt confess with thy mouth the Lord Jesus, and shalt believe in thine heart that God hath raised Him from the dead, thou shalt be saved" (Romans 10:9).

At the bottom of my list of questions and answers I wrote, "Dear Lord, I do love You. How I love to read the Word You have given me! If I am indeed worshiping a false god instead of You—if I am worshiping this false god thinking that it is You—I beg You to let me see the light of Your truth. I beg You, Lord Jesus, do not let me wither away and die because I lack the truth."

Without interference from family, my intensive Bible studies continued with every opportunity. As questions developed during the week I would write them down. Then, with the help of a Bible concordance, a Bible dictionary, and commentaries, I would search for the answers.

Although I knew that the Lord was with me during these times, His presence became especially real one morning. The summer sun was already warming me as I sat on the floor in my bedroom while reading my Bible. Then, taking a moment to look out the window and rest my eyes, I found myself suddenly feeling totally in awe of life. The miracle and wonder and mystery and joy of being alive in this world overwhelmed me. Then I recalled a discussion with Greg about being "born again." As I stared out the window at the beautiful trees and freshly mown lawn, I felt beautiful inside. A feeling of freshness and newness came over me.

"Is this rebirth?" I asked myself. I had been reborn when I had accepted Christ's salvation and forgiveness for my sins at the age of 12, but this was different. Now at the age of 20 I was wanting Jesus Christ to be Lord of my life, to fill my life with His. He wanted to teach me about life and about Himself. He was giving me another chance. He was taking blinders from my eyes and offering me a new look at things. But more than that, He was offering me new life. The Jesus Christ in the Gospel of Matthew jumped off the pages as I read. It was as if He were sitting with me and teaching me.

With confidence I realized that Mormonism and Christianity were two completely different religions. They taught two different gods, two different kinds of Jesus, and two different means of salvation.

I now knew the one and only God and His only begotten Son, who died for my sins. And I knew that believing in Jesus Christ was the only means of salvation. The Lord was definitely dealing with me—but so was another person.

— Chapter 6 —

A Marriage Of Convenience

Well, Master, thou hast said the truth, for there is one God, and there is none other but he; and to love him with all the heart, and with all the understanding, and with all the soul, and with all the strength, and to love his neighbor as himself, is more than all whole burnt offerings and sacrifices.

Mark 12:32,33

The rebirth I experienced that summer morning in 1975 was a second chance for me. It was one more opportunity for me to begin living the way Jesus calls all of us. This new beginning remained strictly a private and personal matter. It had happened between Jesus and me, and it had happened within me. No one knew about my new commitment to Him.

The circumstances under which I was living did not permit me to openly discuss my complete faith in Jesus Christ, and my actions were not necessarily a new demonstration of this experience because I had been trying to live a godly life long before. And because of my living arrangements, my involvement with the Church of Jesus

Christ of Latter-day Saints was not to end immediately.

I also wanted time to grow in my relationship to Jesus and knowledge of Him before I went public with my conversion. Yes, it was an emotional experience, finding new life in Him. But I was assured by the Bible that I had become one with the resurrected Christ whom the Scriptures teach was God and man at once—not a man who became God. From my study I had responded to the message of the Bible—that Christ had died, Christ is risen, and Christ will come again.

I had already made enough mistakes in my young life, and I didn't want this new dedication to Jesus Christ to be another short-lived decision. I knew the basic message of the Bible, but I wanted to know more, to be able to give answers about my beliefs to anyone who asked, particularly my parents. As I worked to establish this foundation, I continued my involvement in the LDS Church, which was soon to increase when I was introduced to a certain young man.

Just two months after moving back into my mother and father's home, I met Ronny. He was 28, never married, and in the same ward as my parents. Six years earlier he had completed his two-year mission for the Mormon Church. He had attended the church's university, Brigham Young University, and he came from an excellent Mormon family. These credentials were impressive in the Mormon Church, and they impressed my family as well.

With only a short time before my second child was due, this new acquaintance was not occupying much of my mind. I was anticipating the birth of another baby, but this anticipation was often interrupted by flowers, cards, and small gifts from Ronny. It was quite clear that our initial meeting was for him more than a casual introduction. Still, I had other things to think about with my baby on his way.

When Joshua arrived, in April of 1975, I welcomed

him with joy and love. My new friend, Ronny, was there to also welcome him. He showed the care and concern for the mother and son that any new father would have— by his visits to the hospital and visits to my parents' home. He was always careful to mention that he wanted to— merely in friendship—check up on me and my sons. And I was intrigued by his apparent genuine concern.

In May my divorce became final, and Ronny and I began dating. I entered that relationship in large part to please my parents, but also because of the encouragement my church friends gave me, and also because I wanted to marry a Mormon man and be sealed in the temple. I also knew that I was a burden as long as I remained with my parents, and that my two children would limit my opportunity for remarriage.

As our relationship was quickly developing, Ronny convinced me that he would consider my two children blessings and that he wanted to father my boys. Desiring to please my parents and give my children a father, I found myself seriously considering marriage to Ronny within two months after we began dating.

Although Ronny was a knowledgeable Mormon concerning the church's moral teachings and commands, and who strictly followed them (even more so than other young men I knew), I began to have strong doubts about another area of his life. There were many times during our courtship when I felt uneasy about the things he would say and do. This forced me to make excuses to continue seeing him: my guilt for having failed at one marriage, my remorse over robbing my two children of their real father, and my past disobedience to the wishes of my parents. The compounding effect of these reasons already made me feel trapped in this new relationship.

Ronny did have many abilities and a lot of refinement— probably too much. That refinement was attractive to some people, especially to those who didn't know him well. As I began spending more time with him, however, his treatment of me became offensive and gave rise for concern.

He believed he could do no wrong, and he humiliated and degraded people to show his importance, power, and control. He degraded me, whom he said he loved, as well as other people.

Emotionally drained following my divorce, I was an easy candidate for his humiliation, probably to satisfy the guilt I felt as a result of the divorce. A typical example of this humiliation took place when he invited me to go swimming one afternoon.

Ronny had been raised on a farm and thought nothing of swimming in irrigation canals. As a city girl, I had never swum in them, and I certainly didn't like the murky water and slimy, moss-covered walls of the canals. When I declined his offer (that was really couched as a challenge), he became belligerent and complained that if I really loved him, I would join him in the water. I had been raised to obey without question my husband or a member of the priesthood in good standing (such as Ronny); I didn't think I had a choice in the matter. So I jumped into the water, hating that first step and fearing the swim.

Fifteen yards upstream was a storage tank. Water filled the tank to within three feet of the rim and then gushed though an enclosed conduit or pipe into the canal. Again, Ronny gave his ultimatum: "If you really love me, Jolene, you'll swim through the tunnel into the storage tank."

"No!" I wasn't about to swim upstream against that strong current of water and fight the bees, wasps, and black widows which lived in the conduit only to enter a claustrophobic storage tank.

"If I do it, will you do it, Jolene?"

"Sure," I laughed, thinking he wouldn't do such a stupid thing. I didn't know that he had practiced to master this feat. Suddenly he was on his way, calling me to follow.

Obediently I made my way though the narrow tunnel. The swift current pushed against me, and the slippery sides made it more treacherous. I was losing my breath and fearing for my life when I barely reached the holding tank before being swept away. There I nearly passed out— but still, there was the return trip. Gasping for air and again fighting the wasps and other insects as they circled around me, I felt nauseous and weak. Why had Ronny wanted me to do this horrible thing? Maybe he just needed me to show him I love him, I told myself. His humiliation of me made me determined to keep the events of the afternoon a secret.

Another incident of humiliation that jeopardized my safety occurred when a discussion turned into an argument while we were traveling on a freeway. In extreme anger, Ronny stopped the truck in the middle of the highway, turned off the engine, walked to the side of the road, and left me there while cars flew past at 70 miles per hour.

Not knowing how to drive the truck, somehow I managed to move it to the side of the road and drive it slowly three miles down the freeway, where I sat for an hour. When Ronny returned, he was filled with anger and threats. And me? I continued trying to justify why I should marry him.

Ronny and I became engaged in July of 1975. Everyone around me had encouraged this step. They felt that it was in my best interest to quickly end the courtship and marry. They offered the obvious reasons, such as living in my own home, having financial support, and letting my parents' life return to normal. I had my own reasons too. I was wrestling with guilt about failing in my first marriage. There was the remorse from robbing my two children of their father. And there was the burden of having disappointed my parents by marrying a non-Mormon. How I longed to once again have that rare smile and wink of approval I had received at a speech festival when they watched me win first place! Perhaps they would again be pleased with me if I married a good Mormon man.

Once Ronny and I were engaged, all I had to do was form a guest list and sew my wedding dress. During this rush of activity, I felt as if family and friends around me had removed all decisions and responsibilities and put me on display. I had somehow stepped out of myself and was now watching a different Jolene being prepared for another marriage. Everyone seemed to be planning for this other Jolene's future—except Jolene herself. All she could do was watch detached from a distance, with only vague anticipation of the event. Communicating with the people who were determining her future was an exercise in futility.

When my beautiful, long wedding dress was completed, it hung in the hallway of my parents' home. But as I would pass it, only a few hours before the wedding, it seemed as though it were meant for someone else. These were not feelings of aloofness, indifference, and preoccupation I was experiencing, but of detachment, neutrality, and numbness.

It was a short ride to the luxurious home of my groom's parents, where the wedding ceremony was to take place— maybe five minutes. In the car with me were my mother and father, and my youngest sister. There was a noticeable silence during the ride, a silence no one wanted to break. Maybe it was apprehension, maybe it was anticipation of the ceremony to come, maybe it was the risk of another marriage. All the while my mind was flashing back to the day of my first marriage. How different my first wedding had been! I had taken charge of its planning and organizing. But more important, I had been completely in love with the man I was to marry.

I remembered, too, the many hours spent designing and sewing that first wedding dress. The sparkling white fabric and the delicate lace had made me feel like a bride. This dress was a soft yellow. It was very beautiful, but suddenly the color took on a new meaning. It was off-white, slightly discolored, impure, tarnished. Was its appearance somehow symbolic of this new phase of my life? Was I making a wise decision?

Only two months after my divorce and with only two months of courtship, Ronny and I were married. The bishop of my parents' ward performed the ceremony. Pictures were taken and hugs exchanged. Gifts were unwrapped and best wishes expressed. But my heart ached through it all. I hadn't planned this event. I hadn't dreamed about this day. Other people had had the dreams and made the plans, and I was to be the one who would live out the consequences. That night I traded my soul for memories that other people had dreamed of, planned for, and prayed for.

— Chapter 7 —

The Masquerade

If any provide not for his own, and especially for those of his own house, he hath denied the faith, and is worse than an infidel.

1 Timothy 5:8

On our wedding night—a night marked by the chill of not being touched by my new husband—I realized how quickly and how far I had turned away from Jesus Christ. In accordance with all my Mormon training and church doctrine, I had submitted my will in obedience to my parents. This act of obedience now meant marriage to a man I did not love, did not respect, and did not like. I did not believe that God had brought Ronny and me together; I did not see in Ronny a partner who would complete me and help me grow closer to God. Nevertheless, I struggled to live up to the commitment I had made. But soon there were signs that frightened me, that caused me to fear for my children's well-being and my own.

Although Ronny had swept my family off their feet, it was now becoming apparent that he had conned his way into our lives. He did come from a home that was respected by all in our ward and from a family of wealth. And he presented himself to my father as a man of wealth who could give his daughter the best of care. Part of his life of deception and trickery was uncovered when he moved me into our first home—a converted milkbarn infested with mice and cockroaches. This was soon followed by his truck, our only transportation, being repossessed. It was not the life that he had promised.

Although I did not enter this marriage with great optimism, believing that all dreams were possible, I did have some modest and realistic expectations. I was not unfamiliar with disappointment, but I was not used to such a high level of this emotion. Furthermore, I should have connected my earlier disappointments in him to his deficient personality traits.

One evening Ronny offered to bathe three-month-old Joshua. Rather than sponging him off with lukewarm water in the bathroom sink, Ronny placed him in the bathtub filled with hot water. As I worked in the kitchen, I heard Josh screaming. Raising my voice to ask what he was doing, Ronny nonchalantly replied that Joshua would not stop crying.

With no confidence in Ronny's answer, I rushed toward the bathroom, where I saw a cloud of steam rising from the water. I lunged for my baby. "What are you doing? Stop it!" I screamed. As he shoved me out of the room, Ronny yelled, "Leave me alone. I can do this." With that he pushed Joshua under the water, holding him there. "I'm just trying to get him to stop crying," Ronny shouted as he came close to drowning my little child.

By this time Ronny seemed crazy and out of control. When he had had enough, he literally threw Joshua at me. Somehow I caught my darling, crying baby, grateful that he was now safe in my arms.

Ronny's response toward my two-year-old was equally alarming. When Justin misbehaved in ways that were typical of any child his age, Ronny reacted by grinding his third knuckle into the soft spot on Justin's head. He insisted on this form of painful discipline, even seeming to enjoy it by inflicting it on Justin for no reason. Occasionally he would lash the boys with a belt, and sometimes I was included as well.

Under the stress of living with this angry man, a man impossible to please, my health began to deteriorate. Emotionally I was being torn apart piece by piece. Headaches filled my nights, and I developed an unrelenting pain deep inside my chest. Many nights I would curl up into a ball and hug my pillow close to me in an attempt to find some comfort and rest.

Comfort was just as hard to find during the waking hours. Now isolated from friends by his demands on me, he had sabotaged all my relationships, activities, and hopes. No more did I have friends for support. Furthermore, sharing the horrible details of my life was not consistent with the Mormon way of hiding one's faults and problems, particularly if it meant ruining my husband's reputation. Thinking for myself and making my own decisions was not an option for me.

Living only two minutes from my parents, I visited them often, trying to find peace and shelter from Ronny's abuse. But never did I share the awful story happening in my home. Eventually I didn't have to because they saw for themselves.

As I lay in a hospital bed, recovering from a physically abusive episode that ended in an attempted strangulation, my parents saw the jeopardy that my children and I were living under. The handprints around my throat told the story. Now my family knew that the one whose insincerity had won their favor was inflicting physical and emotional wounds on their daughter and grandchildren. Bent and twisted, this man had become as evil as sin itself. The attractive appearance and personality of Ronny to those who didn't know him well was a thin covering for the unstable person that he was.

Our first child together was born in May of 1976. On my first night at home from the hospital, I was thrown out of the house naked as my new baby cried quietly to nurse. So that passersby on our brightly lit street wouldn't notice, I hid in the back of our pickup truck until Ronny's fit of madness subsided. After daybreak, I was allowed to enter the converted milkbarn, our home.

In July we moved to a different city and a new job, where he began another masquerade. Maybe this time Ronny would find a secure job, a better place for us to live, and a sense of belonging in the local Mormon ward. After three months he was fired, and we moved again. For almost two years this pattern of life continued. We moved to other homes, other jobs, and other wards. Each time we started anew, and each time we failed.

At home Ronny's iron fist never weakened. He was a member of the church's priesthood, and he believed his family was to bow down and worship him. His super-spirituality filled his prayers as he asked the heavenly Father to cleanse his wife and children of their wrong-doings. He attempted to scare me into total submission to him with stories of Mormon fundamentalists who treated their wives like workhorses. "In the early days of Mormonism," he would say, "husbands even had the right to murder their wives for disobedience and dis-respect." Deeper and deeper I sank into despair, as though I were drowning alone and without hope. Yet I felt powerless to change anything.

My secret Bible studies continued in the midst of this hellish existence. It was these quiet times of Bible reading and prayer with the Lord that helped me keep my sanity. He was my only Friend and source of comfort, for I was not permitted to have contact with anyone in person or by telephone without Ronny's presence.

After a five-month separation I returned to Ronny. It was now November of 1976, and we had moved to Provo,

Utah, a move I hoped would give us a fresh start. But our problems were not caused by geography, and they weren't going to be solved by geography; they were within us. The first snow had fallen and had covered the world with a soft, white blanket. Warm sunlight glistened off the snow and caused the icicles to melt just enough to form little pools of water below the eaves. God seemed to be purifying the earth with this beautiful whiteness.

Inside the faded bungalow were less comforts than might be found in a monk's cell. Boards covered the fireplace, and cold chilled our relationship as well as our bodies. There was no smell of bacon and eggs cooking for breakfast. We had run out of money again and were waiting for the church welfare people to arrive. There was no laughter, no sounds—only the occasional stirring of Benjamin.

Having finished washing the baby's diapers in the bathtub (there was no washing machine) and straightening the sheets on the mattresses which lay on the floor, I sat down to wait for the Relief Society president to come. She was to pick up our grocery list. With the children asleep and Ronny at work, I reached for my Bible. Rather than opening it right away, I stared out the window at the water droplets falling from the eaves.

Quietly I sensed God reminding me, "I will never leave you nor forsake you." There was hope, and it was in His Word. God had not left me even though I had tried to build my relationship with Him on my empty deeds and vain works. He didn't want these things; He wanted *me*. Once again I renewed my dedication to Him.

That morning I read, "All we like sheep have gone astray; we have turned every one to his own way; and the Lord hath laid on him the iniquity of us all" (Isaiah 53:6). "Not by works of righteousness which we have done but according to his mercy he saved us, by the washing of regeneration and renewing of the Holy Ghost, which he shed on us abundantly through Jesus Christ our

Saviour, that being justified by his grace we should be made heirs according to the hope of eternal life" (Titus 3:5-7).

Again I saw confirmation that eternal life comes from believing, not from performing up to any standard. The Holy Spirit was teaching me as I spent time studying the Bible. This was giving me courage and strength to take the next step.

Later that morning I bundled up the kids and pulled them in their wagon through the snow to a telephone at a grocery store. There I called the bishop of our ward and explained my situation to this kind man. He allowed me to pour out the details of our abuse. Recognizing that my husband was very disturbed, he acted immediately, and willingly arranged for me to return to my parents' home. The children and I would fly to Arizona the next morning.

Feeling greatly relieved and hopeful, I hung up the phone and headed home through the snow. I was thankful that the bishop had realized the doctrine of obedience to a husband had been twisted in our home. Whether or not the issue of a temple marriage had entered his mind, he did not hesitate to help. He was genuinely concerned for us and wanted the best for my children and me. I was grateful and thanked God for the way out that He was providing.

Our last night together seemed longer than the night I was thrown out of the house naked. It was past 1:30 in the morning, the time Ronny usually returned home from work. The children were asleep, but I was filled with anxiety about the next day's events and could not sleep. While lying on the blankets and pillows on the floor of the darkened living room, a bright beam of moonlight shone through the curtainless front window.

As I lay there wondering why Ronny was already several hours late, I heard the key in the front door. I knew by the way he handled the knob that he was angry.

When he was inside and had turned on a light, in a nonthreatening way I asked why he had come home so late. As he slowly turned to look at me, his face filled with rage. His eyes were anything but normal, and his manner was inhuman. He threw his coat into the corner and began to yell in a strange chantlike manner. For 15 minutes he screamed at me, and his words were unintelligible. As the shouting continued, I held my ears, crying and begging him to stop.

At this point, I felt as if I were seeing mysterious things. The room seemed to be filled with a strange and heavy air which I could feel surrounding and suffocating me, but Ronny didn't seem to notice this stifling atmosphere. As I looked at him I saw a strange, unnatural expression cross his face. It was almost a smile, yet it was ghastly and distorted. Then the thick air began to move. The breeze gained speed and was soon circling the room. For several minutes the air whipped around the room at an enormous speed, only to stop abruptly.

Now standing directly in front of me, my husband commanded me to kneel and pray. This request was not unusual. Ronny had always been fanatical about the rituals of the church. He was concerned about doing the "right things" and would not go to bed at night until he prayed. These prayers to the "high and gracious heavenly Father" were not really prayers but sermons to me. He would preach to me about obedience and submission to the husband I had married. Even tonight, Ronny did not break his habit of nightly prayer.

I replied that I wouldn't pray with him but would kneel as he had instructed. As he began to pray I watched him because I was afraid of what he might do if I shut my eyes. I don't remember any of his words. I was shaking with fear and too aware that this was not the Ronny I knew. Something was very wrong.

Terrified, I began to pray, first silently and then aloud. I claimed Christ as my Savior and demanded that the oppression be lifted from Ronny and from this room at once. Then, as if none of this strangeness had occurred, Ronny collapsed onto the blankets on the floor and was asleep in minutes.

My eyes did not close the rest of the night. Instead, I lay awake silently praying, thanking God for His protection and rejoicing in His promise: "Weeping may endure for a night, but joy cometh in the morning" (Psalm 30:5). God had protected my children and me, and I was thankful. Ronny's behavior was not of this world but demonic, I have since come to understand.

There was joy the next morning. Before Ronny left for work, I told him without details that I would be returning to Arizona with the children. I couldn't risk having him stand in my way. He listened calmly, and probably didn't believe me. I had never done anything against his will, but then I had never been pushed to this extreme. We were in danger as long as we were living with him. Escape was a high priority.

Soon after Ronny left for work, the bishop arrived to take us to the airport. In only a few hours we would be in Arizona with people who cared for us and loved us. There I would make some major decisions about my future based on the lessons I had learned.

During our flight to Arizona, thoughts of our future occupied my mind. Life for a single mother of three children would not be easy. I had married Greg because I loved him. I had married Ronny to please other people and to provide a father for my sons. Now, more than anything, I wanted to live a life pleasing to God.

— Chapter 8 —

Between Two Worlds

If ye be reproached for the name of Christ, happy are ye, for the spirit of glory and of God resteth upon you; on their part he is evil spoken of, but on your part he is glorified.

1 Peter 4:14

Here we go again, I thought to myself. It was August of 1977. Once again I was being wheeled down a hospital corridor to the labor rooms. The pains were coming every four minutes, and they were lasting for 45 to 55 seconds.

As I slipped into the labor bed and pulled the cold sheets up around my neck, I began to prepare for the journey. As I had done during each previous delivery, today I would take an imaginary trip to somewhere far away, to somewhere that was peaceful and beautiful. This time I chose a long country road lined with majestic oak trees. There would not be any people in this dream—only God and me. His company would give me a serene journey and help for the strenuous hours ahead.

The doctor had confirmed my pregnancy in February, three weeks after I had returned home from Utah. Driving home from his office with tears streaming down my cheeks, I searched for answers to my trying situation. For what higher reason was I pregnant? How could this timing be right? A fourth pregnancy—and I was alone again. There wasn't a husband to share the "oohs" and "aahs" with or help me choose a name. And there wasn't anyone's hand to hold. Alone—that's not what I wanted for myself, yet it seemed my fate.

As I thought about these things, I suddenly felt ashamed and ungrateful. God was again performing a miracle of new life inside me, and I was responding with a self-pitying why-me attitude. I determined that no matter how difficult this pregnancy might be, I would find joy in it. Soon the Lord blessed me with another beautiful baby boy, Brandon, and I returned from the hospital to four more months with my parents.

Those months in waiting were marked by a time of significant spiritual growth, a time of learning to trust the Lord with every need and every decision. It was a time when I learned much about the spiritual disciplines of prayer, meditation, study, confession, and worship.

My parents and I had been looking for a home I could call my own, and at last we found a place. Moving day would be two weeks before Christmas, and I was excited about sharing Christmas with my own little family. We could trim a tree, decorate cookies, and make our own wrapping paper with finger paint and butcher paper. It would be a joyous celebration of the birth of Jesus and of being on my own.

I had prayed long for this time when my children and I would have our own little independence day, when we could live in our own house. But I soon realized that I was still dependent on the LDS Church, although I could not accept many of their doctrines anymore.

The members of my ward had welcomed me when I returned from Utah. They had kindly and graciously helped me back to a normal way of life after I left Ronny.

But now I found myself in a dilemma between taking a stand for Jesus Christ and disappointing these Latter-day Saints who had helped me get a new start in Arizona.

Their help did not end the week I returned, but continued for months, for which I am grateful. As an unemployed, single mother, I was tightly bound to them. Their kindness, the feeling they gave that I was part of a community, the security I felt among them, the memories of growing up in the faith—all of these things kept me closely tied to the Mormon Church even though I wanted to break away.

As the holiday season began, I poured my time and energy into decorating, baking, and enjoying the festivities of Christmas. In the midst of this busyness my desire to be involved in a Christian church grew. However, when Sunday came, I would find some reason why I couldn't attend this Sunday, and vow to attend the new church the following week.

Also dampening the Christmas joy was the fact that I could not support myself and my children without working outside the home. My only income was the child support check, with which Greg was as reliable as Ronny was unreliable. When Greg's check arrived, the money was used only for the children. With reservation but not knowing where else to turn, I sought advice from my parents. Their answer was as expected—church welfare. How I hated the thought! It brought back memories of my second marriage, baggage that I wanted to leave behind.

For three more weeks I read the want ads daily and asked everyone about available jobs. Having no previous experience, I was unable to find a job. My parents could not offer complete financial assistance, and child support did not cover all my expenses. Backed against the wall, I accepted church welfare and with it further commitments to the Mormon Church.

Having swallowed my pride in deciding to accept the

church's assistance, I again felt the ease of receiving its help. My parents simply made a phone call, and before I knew it my needs were taken care of. While this existence may sound carefree and attractive, it required work for the church in return for its generosity, quite unlike welfare from the government.

Once again I was attending church meetings and working long hours at the church welfare center, though not dedicated to the church's teachings. Many times I felt as if I were caught in a web, and the harder I fought, the more entangled I became.

One of my continuing prayers was that I could have a home of my own where I would be free of all obligations to the Mormon Church and its influence. But somehow that prayer brought even deeper involvement in the church.

Like almost every day, I sat down for my morning Bible study. This was a practice I had continued while still involved in the life of the Mormon Church. But this morning as I read, the Scriptures seemed written especially for me. My heart pounded as I read the words of Paul calling God's servants to teach people who opposed them so that "they may recover themselves out of the snare of the devil" (2 Timothy 2:26). He described the danger and tragedy of people who are "ever learning and never able to come to the knowledge of the truth" (2 Timothy 3:7). He showed that "all that will live godly in Christ Jesus shall suffer persecution," and he encouraged me to continue "in the things which thou hast learned and hast been assured of, knowing of whom thou hast learned them" (2 Timothy 3:12,14). Paul also charged me to honor the "holy Scriptures, which are able to make thee wise unto salvation through faith which is in Christ Jesus" (2 Timothy 3:15).

As I read 2 Timothy several times that morning, God strengthened my faith and my resolve to again examine the Mormon doctrine. Instead of sitting quietly in my

Mormon Sunday school classes, I began to ask questions of my teachers—lots of them. These were honest questions to which I had found answers in my Bible study time, but I wanted answers from Mormon teachers.

But the answers were not forthcoming. The responses were always vague and indirect. Not once did I receive an answer based on the authority of Scripture. Their approach was "Well, perhaps" or "Personally, I believe...." On one occasion the teacher asked me to remember my question until after class, when we would have more time to discuss it. My suspicions that he was hoping I would forget the matter were confirmed. After class he suddenly remembered that he had something important to do.

Although my questioning didn't reap many satisfying answers, I discovered that other people had questions too. Through my church activities I met two young LDS men and we became good friends. In our discussions about the church, I was surprised to find that neither of them believed any of the Mormon doctrine and teachings. Like me, their questions were always left unanswered. Yet they remained in the church because their social needs were met by its programs. More precisely, one belonged for his mother's sake and the other had joined to keep his girlfriend from ending their relationship. They therefore remained active and exemplary LDS men despite the fact that they believed nothing the church taught.

My thirst for the Bible increased my desire to grow in the Christian life and leave the Church of Jesus Christ of Latter-day Saints and its influence. I was tired of living a Mormon life as a Christian. It seemed that everywhere I turned there was a Mormon watching my life. My parents, my sisters, the bishop, the stake president, the visiting teachers, the home teachers, and the Sunday school teachers all seemed to know my activities, my plans, and my contacts. At every turn there was someone watching my life. Boxed in and overwhelmed with a sense of despair, I was nearing the point where I would trade my security to live as a Christian.

Disappointed in my weaknesses, I needed strength to take a stand for what was right. I wanted to serve the Lord, but I still needed financial help, and the Mormon Church was providing it. But I wanted to free myself from its clutches.

On my knees and weeping, I cried to God for a way out. I seemed to have exchanged the imprisonment of a marriage for the imprisonment by the church. Depressed, days would pass when I wouldn't change from bathrobe to clothes. The four children and I stayed inside with the doors locked and the shades drawn.

I knew that this could not go on forever, and yet I was frightened by my own thoughts and feelings. From what my family and friends could see, I was doing fine. But once alone, I cried for hours. When I wasn't crying I was praying that God would give me the courage to leave Mormonism. And that courage was soon to come in an unexpected way.

— *Chapter 9* —

Between Two Families

He that loveth father or mother more than me is not worthy of me.

Matthew 10:37

Springtime was coming, and with it the promise of new life. The fruit trees' delicate buds, the robins' spotted eggs, and the colorful flowers brought to the world a feeling of newness. It was time for spring cleaning. I opened the curtains and washed the windows. The children helped me scrub floors and clean closets. My small sons giggled and their little eyes sparkled as they began to see new hope in their mommy. Since the new year began, God seemed to be giving me, as well as His world, a bright start.

Part of this new beginning can be found in the end of my first marriage. Since our divorce, in May of 1975, Greg had been a faithful and loving father to his children. Except for the times during my marriage to Ronny when we were living far from the Phoenix area, Greg saw his children every Saturday.

As for me, Ronny had forbidden me to do anything but stick my head out the door when Greg came for the

children. And when I was living with my parents, they
watched that he didn't say anything to me when he picked
up Justin and Joshua.

Despite these attentive guards, Greg had managed again
and again to leave me with the words, "I love you dearly.
I'm still praying for you. It's going to be okay, Jolene."

Away from the watchful eye of family and living in
my own house, I was free to invite Greg in when he picked
up the boys. Our basic, "How have you been?" conversations were the beginning of a renewed relationship. It
wasn't long before Greg was inviting me to go on his
Saturday outings with our sons. Sometimes he stayed at
the house for the day. Soon Greg felt free to ask, "Can
I come by Wednesday night?" When I didn't hesitate to
say "Sure," he asked about Thursday night as well—
and he received the same wholehearted "Sure." This
pattern developed into regular stops in the morning before
work: "Do you need anything today, Jolene?" And in
the evening after work: "Just wanted to make sure you're
doing okay."

This time together was real happiness. I was ecstatic.
I had never stopped loving Greg and had prayed that
somehow he would come back, but I didn't expect those
prayers to be answered—at least in the way I wanted them
answered.

Greg had told me on many occasions that he was also
praying for me, and I was encouraged that he had not
remarried. Still, I was afraid to believe (not wanting to
be disappointed) that he might someday return. Now I
found myself more in love with Greg than ever. He was
always a man I could respect and trust, and he understood
me better than anyone else.

Furthermore, Greg was the only person in my life who
had ever truly cared about my soul. It was Greg who
discipled me. It was he who had encouraged me to accept
Jesus as a Friend and Savior.

The best part of Greg's visits were the many hours we

spent reading God's Word. He would bring me books and tapes that helped in my Bible study and would answer my questions about Mormonism and the Bible. If we came upon a question he couldn't answer, he would search until he found an explanation. We were able to laugh and cry together as our Lord Jesus Christ began to put the pieces of our lives together again.

One Saturday morning in February, Greg and I began loading sandwiches, potato salad, cookies, and fruit into the picnic basket. We climbed into the car with Justin, Joshua, Benjamin, and Brandon, and the adventure began. Our destination was the annual hot-air balloon competition near Tempe, Arizona.

We weren't the first people to arrive. Excitement already filled the air. The bright reds, yellows, and blues of the big balloons stood in vivid contrast to the desert landscape and pale sky. At roadside stands people sold programs, cold drinks, cotton candy, and souvenirs. In the background, bands played Sousa marches and fifties songs. The laughter and fun were contagious.

Greg and I quickly claimed a patch of ground at the top of one of the gentle hills near a small duck pond. We had a perfect view of all the festivity. We shared the balloonists' enthusiasm and the kids' sense of joyous freedom. As we watched our older boys roll down the grassy hill and feed their sandwiches to the ducks, Greg and I basked in a sense of contentment and pleasure of each other's company.

"Jolene, it's so right for us to be together like this. And it's so comfortable and easy. . . ."

As I watched the boys run around and heard their giggles, I had to agree with Greg. It indeed seemed very natural and right for the six of us to be sharing this day.

"I would like to make this arrangement more permanent. I would like us to be a family once again. Jolene, I'd like you to be my wife again."

With tears of joy and a heart full of thankfulness to

God, I accepted Greg's proposal. With our arms around each other, we thanked God for once again bringing us together. "Lord," I prayed, "thank You for blessing us with a love that has lasted. Thank You for bringing us through the storms of the past three years. And thank You for the precious gift of Greg's love. Help me to be a good wife and help us to rely on You each step of the way."

We both knew the consequences of our remarriage. Without a doubt my family would disown me, and our friends would be skeptical. The road ahead could be rough and quite lonely. We were concerned for the children, and we wanted what was best for them. We realized that they too had felt the pain of the past few years. There was the possibility that our remarriage could bring more hurt into our lives and the lives of the children.

The most important issue of remarriage was our relationship with God. As much as I wanted to be with Greg as his wife, I first wanted the assurance that I was right with the Lord and relying on Him for help, strength, and guidance. And I wanted to enter into our remarriage aware of the difficulties we would face. Therefore we decided to begin marital and spiritual counseling before we shared our plans with anyone.

For two months Greg and I met two to three nights a week for counseling with two of our pastors. After several weeks of self-examination and personal and spiritual growth, Greg and I were supported by our pastors in our desire to remarry. We also believed that God's blessing was on our union, so a day in April was set for our remarriage. The next step was to share our plans with family and friends.

Breaking the news of our plans for remarriage to my father was as difficult as I had imagined. Words such as "ungrateful," "undeserving," and "untrustworthy" were thrown at me. This time, though, there was not the sharp pain I had felt whenever I had disappointed my father before. I knew that this time I was doing the will of my heavenly Father. And instead of the emptiness, guilt, and shame that such attacks had once brought, I felt a sweet joy and gentle pride, for I had stood up for what I believed and wanted. This was a freeing moment. However, tears streamed down my cheeks as I pleaded with my father to understand and to keep loving me.

When the confrontation was over, so was my relationship with my family. Finally I had expressed my feelings and shared my beliefs, and it had cost me dearly. My father disowned me. I was despised and unwelcome in his home. I was an outcast, the black sheep of the family. My mother did not repeat my father's words to me, but she made clear her disappointment and reminded me of her duty to stand by my father all the way because he held the priesthood.

My parents did not attend our wedding at Grace Community Church, but Greg's parents were there. There we celebrated God's grace, His forgiveness, His healing, and His love. Now the rebuilding of a marriage would begin as Greg and I established our home.

God blessed in many ways our efforts to walk with Him. He blessed us with a love for each other and a joy-filled marriage that could only come from Him. The year after we were married we were blessed with a new home which we designed and constructed. But more important, He blessed us spiritually through His Word and gave us a boldness to share what we learned with others, particularly those in the Church of Jesus Christ of Latter-day Saints.

During our city's bicentennial celebration in early 1980, I met Jim Robertson. He and his wife, Judy, were the leaders of an organization called Concerned Christians. Their purpose was to inform the Mormon community of the false foundation of their faith and the truth found in the Bible alone. Concerned Christians was formed by people of various denominations, some of whom are former Mormons who have come to know Jesus as their Lord and Savior.

Greg and I soon began attending weekly meetings of Concerned Christians. During one meeting I realized that I was still a member of the Mormon Church. Having claimed Jesus as my Savior, I wanted to be a member of His church alone. So I composed a letter to the Mormon Church president in Salt Lake City, Spencer Kimball, and requested that my name be removed from the church records.

Although I knew that this was right, it would be another black mark next to my name, widening the gap between my family and me. But strengthened and supported in that act by my husband, by Christian friends, and by the Lord, I had my name removed from the Mormon records. My family was devastated. They expressed their displeasure in silence and separation. And this separation was to be forever.

— *Chapter 10* —

Going Public

Where your treasure is, there will your heart be also.

Luke 12:34

My heart pounded fiercely as I was introduced. Anticipation had been building within me as Jim Robertson had asked me weeks earlier to speak at a seminar on Mormonism. I was to explain the history, teachings, and doctrines of the Church of Jesus Christ of Latter-day Saints. I accepted the opportunity and spent many hours studying and praying in preparation for this evening. The audience would be composed of Christians concerned about their Mormon neighbors and some Mormons who might publicly seek to discredit those who spoke.

Concerned Christians gave Greg and me many opportunities to speak to Mormon people who were searching for more than the church's way of life. By our testimony to the gospel of Christ, we hoped people would be freed from doctrine that stressed the importance of works and the appearance of a perfect family. And because of our openness, many Mormons spoke to us about their emptiness after many years of devotion and sacrifice to the church.

Those who recognized that the Mormon way of striving for perfection and godhood leads nowhere often accepted the freeing invitation of Christ: "Come unto me, all ye that labor and are heavy laden, and I will give you rest. Take my yoke upon you and learn of me, for I am meek and lowly in heart, and ye shall find rest unto your souls. For my yoke is easy and my burden is light" (Matthew 11:28-30). Just as these Jewish leaders to whom Jesus was talking were caught up in a false form of godliness called legalism, so are those who remain in the Mormon Church.

Now as I waited for my cue, I was trying to control my fear of speaking to a large audience. A little off-balance because of being seven months pregnant, would I trip on the way to the podium? Would I make it through my conversion experience and the story of God's grace without crying? I took a deep breath, stood up slowly, and carefully crossed the stage to the microphone. I wanted so much for the Lord to use my words in a way that would make Mormons receptive to the gospel.

As I shared my story with a sea of unfamiliar faces, I continued to silently thank God for what He had done in my life in two short years. "Jesus, the Good Shepherd, did indeed find one like a sheep that had gone astray. He found me frustrated and trapped in a world of pressure and confusion and false security. He saw me struggling to be perfect. He watched me labor under the Mormon Church's call to perform, under an exhausting schedule that didn't permit time for reflection, under a futile striving after nothing. He asked me to give up my yoke of elaborate legalism, regulations, and performance as the means of gaining acceptance and salvation, and instead to simply accept Him. With the salvation from sin He imparts came rest for my soul, rest I never had as a Mormon."

As I looked into the tear-filled eyes of the people in

the audience, I prayed that people would be moved to question the Mormon teachings they had long believed. I prayed that God would raise doubts about the Mormon faith and cause people to examine the claims of Jesus Christ. I wanted those in the audience who did not know Him as Savior to experience His freeing love and sure salvation.

"Just as God saw me struggle, He is watching some of you strive for perfection that we are unable to achieve. He is watching you live according to a set of rules that can never provide your salvation. And as you strive, you do so ignoring the salvation from sin that only Jesus Christ can provide. Don't miss it. He asks you today, just as He asked me, to accept Him and experience the abundant and eternal life."

Standing before the audience, I realized anew the true purpose of life. I had not come to this earth because I had been noble and faithful in a preexistent state and to prove myself worthy of becoming a god in the afterlife. This life on earth was not a test where my performance would determine my future godhood. Instead, I had been born on this earth a sinner. And my purpose was to glorify God and tell of the forgiveness and salvation from sin available in Christ Jesus.

Several speakers spoke that night, presenting the differences between Mormonism and Christianity. At the end we spent several hours with Mormons who were shocked by our stories and wanted to know more. They were searching for truth and meaning in their lives, and they wanted to know how we had been able to break away from the Mormon Church.

As Greg and I drove home, I shared with him some of my thoughts from earlier in the evening. "I realized again, Greg, that I want to be open to the Lord and sensitive to His leading. I want Him to use me as an example of the change that takes place when we accept Him as our Lord and Savior."

"Jolene, if that is your true desire—and I'm sure it is—then we need to study the Bible more than ever. The Lord can't use us if we aren't learning His Word and applying it to our lives."

"I agree." I spoke softly, thinking about the implications of Greg's statement.

"You know, Jolene, we've come to a place in our lives where we need to be watchful."

"Watchful?" I asked.

"Yes. For example, just think about all the earthly possessions we've accumulated recently. They are one of many things that could cause us to take our eyes off Jesus and ruin our effectiveness for Him. And think about the way God seems to be using us as we share our story. If we begin to feel that the ministry is ours alone and that its success is our doing, we'll get tripped up by pride."

I sighed in agreement. Greg was right.

He added, "Now that Satan knows your heart and goals for your ministry, he'll try anything to get you off-track as you work to share the news of Jesus."

Thinking about what Greg said, I felt a twinge of guilt—and rightfully so. I was quite proud of my appearance and possessions. And only recently had this pride begun to build around things such as new cars, large homes, stylish clothes, and social status. I really did need to be watchful. Satan could find a weakness in my life when I took my eyes off Jesus.

Greg continued, "I'm not saying that the earthly security we're now enjoying will make us stumble. Money doesn't have to cause selfishness and pride. I am saying, however, that because we're so young and because we've gained these assets so fast, we must be cautious."

Greg was right. I thought of my parents. They had gained their wealth through many years of hard work and being thrifty. My father had advanced from a construction company workman to a partnership in a successful business. That success, however, had taken many years.

But it seemed that Greg and I had it all by the time he was 26 and I was 23. Now I hoped that we would be able to handle the responsibilities and challenges that came with the financial comfort we were enjoying.

We drove on in silence, both aware of the seriousness of our conversation. Greg pulled into the circular driveway of our home and parked the car. Turning to face me, he took my hand and gently squeezed it.

"I love the Lord with all my heart, and I love you, Jolene. And I want us to dedicate our lives to the Lord we love. I also want us to devote our lives to reach Mormon people who don't yet know Jesus. They are truly lost. They need those who understand their world and can share God's Word with them.

"God, thank You for Your marvelous plan of salvation. Thank You for loving us even though we fall short of being the people You call us to be. Thank You for sending Your Son to die for us so that we can be Your children. Thank You, too, for the blessing of our marriage and for the ministry You have called us to. I pray, Father God, that we be given strength, discernment, and wisdom as we share Your story and our own experience. We truly want to serve You, Father. Help us to love You with all our hearts and all our minds. We dedicate our lives to You. Amen."

As the months quickly passed, our spiritual lives matured as we attended the worship services and activities at Grace Community Church in Tempe, Arizona. We became active in the Young Marrieds Class, and we taught the AWANA class to eight- and nine-year-old boys on Wednesday evenings. Once a week Greg met with other men for Bible study and breakfast, and I attended weekly meetings at a women's Bible study. Yet there was still time for our personal and family life.

By now there were all kinds of evidence that indicated that God had reconciled us to Himself and we to each other. It was a quiet December morning, and I remember the crystal blue and the soft white puffs of the early-morning sky. The cool, crisp air made me shiver as I picked up the newspaper from the front porch. "What a beautiful day for a birthday!" I exclaimed. It was 1980. Today I turned 24.

In the house, Greg was almost ready for work. The boys were seated in front of the television set, spellbound by their favorite cartoon show. Jennifer, now two months old, was warmly bundled in her bassinet. She breathed softly as she slept.

As I considered the scene, I quietly wondered, "Who could ask for more?"

The business that Greg had started with his brother two years earlier had been an overnight success. It provided both families with a very comfortable lifestyle. I had been able to spend many hours at drapery shops, carpet and tile companies, wallpaper stores, and furniture warehouses picking out colors and styles to decorate our new country home. Its elegant Spanish design with its hues of blue, brown, and beige had just the flavor of Old Mexico that we wanted.

Not only had we been blessed financially, but because of our ministry we had also met many Christians who became our friends. Greg and I both felt that God had given us some of life's most precious gifts as we considered our family, our home, our church, and our friends.

As Greg walked out the door, he mysteriously told me to be dressed and ready to go with him in an hour.

"Okay, I'll be ready," I answered, wondering what he was up to.

He hurried toward the car with a mischievous grin on his face. "See ya later," he called.

I finished the breakfast dishes and straightened the kitchen in a hurry. I was anxious to be ready when Greg returned. As I put the finishing touches on my makeup and adjusted my outfit, Greg called from the garage, "Jolene! Come here—quick! I have something to show you!"

Thinking that he must have my birthday present, I hurried to the garage. As I ran through the door, my heart skipped a beat. There in place of my old car was a new burgundy Corvette!

"Happy birthday, Honey. Bet you never thought you'd own one of these!"

I couldn't believe what I was seeing, because Greg and I had always shared the wild dream of owning a Corvette. Now, as I sat in the plushly upholstered driver's seat, I couldn't believe that the car was really mine. This was a birthday I would never forget!

— *Chapter 11* —

A House Divided

I am come to send fire on the earth.... The father shall
be divided against the son, and the son against the father;
the mother against the daughter, and the daughter against
the mother.

Luke 12:49,53

As 1981 began, Greg's business continued to prosper.
We were able to spend more time alone together and more
time with our children. We planted trees and worked in
the garden at our new home. We traveled, camped, fished,
and shared picnic lunches and afternoons of baseball at
the local park.

Ironically, as our family grew closer, there was a
growing feeling of loneliness inside me that I could not
ignore. Disowned by my family because I renounced the
Mormon faith, they could no longer include me in their
lives. They knew I still wanted to be part of them, but
they rejected me. Whenever I was with them, they seemed
nervous and insecure, and never wanted to discuss what
divided us.

Wanting answers to my questions, I decided to telephone

my sister, Sandra, for an explanation to ease my nagging loneliness. I quickly realized that rebuilding a relationship with my family would be harder than I thought.

"Why don't you call or come over and visit anymore?" I didn't waste any time getting to the reason for my call.

After hesitating for a few moments, she answered, "I have my family to take care of. I can't be worried about you and your family. You've made your decision, Jolene, and it's not up to me to convince you that you're wrong. You've obviously closed your mind to anything we might say."

She really hadn't answered my question, so I asked again. "Why don't you call or come over anymore?"

Again, avoiding the real issue but this time responding in a much stronger voice, Sandra answered, "Jolene, I am a very busy person. I have a family to care for, church meetings to attend, and church jobs to do. If you hadn't quit the church, you too would be busy and wouldn't have time to feel sorry for yourself."

"I'm not sitting around with nothing to do. And I'm definitely not feeling sorry for myself," I said, irritated by her accusation.

"Yes, you are! And if you don't realize it now, you are going to end up being very unhappy."

Annoyed by my sister's lecturing, I simply said, "I'm sorry I bothered you. Goodbye." Then I hung up the phone.

I was stunned by my reaction to Sandra. Our conversation did not go the way I had desired or predicted. It had begun as a sincere attempt to find some honest answers to my questions. But the forces and emotions of the conversation continued to deteriorate with each question and answer, beginning with the blame I was to accept for our break in communication and association.

But there was another reason that may have put our conversation on edge that she never mentioned. Months before, when I had requested the removal of my name from the Mormon records, I became an apostate member of my family's church. Now I was to be regarded as one unable to accept the "truth" of the Mormon doctrine, an untouchable.

In order to participate in the temple, my family had to be able to say no when asked, "Do you associate with any apostate members of the Church of Jesus Christ of Latter-day Saints?" (Although my family did communicate with me from time to time, apparently the connection was not close enough or frequent enough to mean that they were "associating" with me.)

Church constraints kept my family from reaching out to me. And because it did not look like I was going to change my ways, my family came to the conclusion that their attempts to relate to me and my family were pointless. When Greg and I reached out to them, we felt they questioned our motives. This seeming distrust and the growing isolation hurt me deeply.

One evening I tried to express my heartache to my mother. Greg and his father were away on a weekend hunting trip, so there was more opportunity for me to talk with my mother. I hoped that since we would be alone, she would be more open with me as we discussed our families.

"I know it's hard for Sandra and Ellen to accept me," I began, "but why do they keep me completely out of their lives? Why do they avoid me? They take turns babysitting for each other when they have doctors' appointments or church meetings. I have children too, and I'd enjoy helping them out. But I'm never asked. My children are even left out of birthday parties and holiday events. Why?"

Resolving conflict within a family is never easy, and my mother's body language was indicating that she was uncomfortable with my questions. Possibly wanting to protect my sisters, she answered, "Well, you live so far away."

"No, I don't. I'm no farther away from them than they are from each other."

"Well, maybe they do try to reach you and can't get hold of you."

"No, Mother, that isn't it either, and I think you know it. It's because I'm not a Mormon anymore, isn't it? They aren't comfortable talking to me, are they?"

"Well," she hesitated, "I guess that's true. You've changed, and they don't know how to deal with you. You talk about Jesus so much that I guess they think you're too fanatical."

"Fanatical!" I exclaimed. "Why is talking about Jesus fanatical?"

"Well, it isn't, except you do it in a way that they don't know how to deal with. It makes them uneasy."

"Mother, Jesus is the center of my life. I can't stop talking about Him just so my sisters will talk to me."

"Jolene, this is hard on all of us. You were raised an LDS girl. You were the strongest one, the most spiritual of all three of you girls. I just don't know what happened. It may take a long time for any of us to accept what you've done."

As I drove back to my home a nauseous feeling because of our conflict came over me. How could she reject Jesus so completely? Didn't she see what she was doing? And why couldn't my sisters still be my sisters?

In spite of the avoidance by my parents and sisters, they were communicating a message of displeasure and rejection. But at the same time, I believed that even though we had these differences, our total relationship didn't have to be terminated.

My mother was able to talk to me, but I realized that the tie between mother and daughter is closer than that between sisters. Still, I couldn't understand why my family didn't love me simply because I was their daughter, their sister. I desperately wanted them to understand that I shouldn't have to be exactly like them for them to love me, but they weren't able to do this. The emptiness inside me burned white-hot.

Not ready to see my ties with my family cut off forever, I wanted more than ever to be able to talk with them, to share what I had learned about Jesus and how He had helped me cope with the hell of my second marriage— even how He helps me with life's day-to-day struggles. I wanted to tell them how Jesus had become real in my life: He was my personal Friend, not a remote heavenly being. But, as is often the case, the bridges of communication with family are most narrow and the walls of protection most high.

One night shortly after my conversation with my mother, the phone rang as I was drifting off to sleep. "Oh, hi, Mom," I said drowsily.

"We'll be having family night on Monday. Are you, Greg, and the kids coming?" she asked.

Turning to Greg, I whispered, "How about Monday night? A Family Home Evening, okay?"

"Sure," he replied in a way that suggested he really wasn't too interested in going or answering my question.

I told my mother to expect us and then said goodbye.

"Are you sure you want to go?" Greg asked.

"No, I'm not sure," I said, already regretting my answer. Then I turned away to hide my tears.

When we were first married we had begun attending Family Home Evenings at my parents' home. But now, because of the strained relationships between families, the evening would not be an easy one.

Family Home Evenings were designed to encourage close family ties. The evenings involved church lessons, church hymns, a game or two, and plenty of time for socializing. Although unstructured, this time for talking inevitably focused on life in the Mormon Church.

Since Greg and I were not involved in the Mormon Church, we were socially uncomfortable at these affairs. The lessons and songs were omitted when we attended,

I suppose as an accommodation to us, which we never requested. All that was left after dinner were games and plenty of time for socializing, but the conversation always centered on Mormonism. Greg and I couldn't help but feel like outsiders looking in on this world of which we would never be a part. And because of our involvement with Concerned Christians, their distrust of us was great.

As we listened to the different ones who led our Family Home Evening, I wished they knew the Savior so they wouldn't be striving to save themselves. They were very much committed to the church and had felt the "burning in the bosom," their subjective confirmation of the truth of their doctrine. They believed in the church's teachings and its prophets, and they would defend Mormonism whatever the cost. As the "anti-Mormon groups" emerged, my family wondered how anyone could not see that the Mormons were Christian.

As my family learned more of our involvement with Concerned Christians, their distrust and suspicion became dark clouds over the evening. From then on, every Monday night would be difficult, but I accepted the next invitation anyway. I loved my family and was not going to give them the chance to blame me for the breakdown of communication. I didn't want to reject them though they were avoiding me. Instead, I wanted to love them in spite of the pain.

When the next Monday night came, Greg and I felt the isolation more than ever. It couldn't have been more effective if we had had a communicable disease. We entered my parents' home to a room full of people who were too busy to notice our arrival. Feeling uneasy about our place in the group, we eventually found our places around the table. As food was passed from person to person, conversation continued all around us, but no one acknowledged our presence. Finally, as though stunned to see me there, my older sister managed a "Hi, Jo," and then resumed her conversation with my mother.

Greg and I ate dinner, feeling like ghosts that people simply couldn't see. When we tried to add something to a conversation, our words went unnoticed.

After dinner the men took their usual place in the family room. There they exchanged hunting stories and business frustrations. The women began to clear the table of dishes. As I walked from the dining room to the kitchen, I passed my sisters and my mother. The blank expressions on their faces made me want to scream, "Hey, I'm here! It's me, Jolene! Remember me? I'm your sister, your daughter." I knew that if Greg and I didn't leave now, I would say something that I might later regret. Without finishing the dishes, I gathered the children, grabbed Greg's arm, and said one goodbye.

Once in the car, I felt my bottled-up emotions come uncorked. "I'm never going back!" I cried. "That's it! I'm through!"

My outburst was met by total silence. My normally active, noisy children were completely quiet. I turned to look at them and saw tiny teardrops rolling down their small cheeks. Glancing in Greg's direction, I saw that he was feeling the same hurt and rejection I was. He placed his hand on my knee to indicate he understood and that we were in this together. Now more than ever, I could see that my acceptance of Jesus Christ was an embarrassment to my family. I sat in the darkness of the car and trembled beneath the intense hurt I was feeling. The childhood nightmare of being separated from one's parents was now a horrible reality.

I wasn't ready to lose my family. I prayed earnestly for my parents, my brother, and my sisters. I wanted God to mend the broken relationships. I wanted to share with them my hurts and sorrows and to comfort them in theirs. Ellen and her husband had been in a terrible car accident. Sandra had lost a child while he was napping. I longed to be with them during this difficult time, but their hearts were closed to me. My brother, Jim, and his wife had not been able to have the children they so desperately wanted. How I wished to encourage them and share my children with them! Again, they couldn't hear my words or be close to my children.

During this time I gained a clearer understanding of the pain and rejection that Christ must have faced. He too was rejected by those He loved.

Quiet walks at dusk gave me the time I needed to sort out these feelings and understand the emotions which battled inside me. Dressed in my old, faded jogging suit, I walked down dirt roads past small farms just outside our suburban neighborhood. Eventually I came to nothing but empty fields for as far as I could see. As I walked along, I held my hands tightly inside the warm kangaroo pocket of my sweatshirt and enjoyed the tranquility of the surrounding area. I was ready to think and talk to God. A frequent starting point for these mental wanderings was my Mormon training.

Since childhood, I had planned to marry a Mormon man in a Mormon temple. We would raise Mormon children, be involved in the Mormon Church, and live together happily ever after as we worked toward the Mormon reward of godhood. I had been taught that such a life of commitment and obedience to the Mormon Church brought honor and fulfillment, and I had expected nothing out of life except this Mormon version of "happily ever after." When my own experience didn't conform to this Mormon scenario, I was ill-prepared for the reality of life with its hardships, disappointments, decisions, and struggles. In my emptiness and puzzlement I turned to Jesus Christ.

On one particular evening, I prayed aloud to Jesus as I walked: "Lord, please take away the painful emptiness that I feel without my family. Fill the void that's left since they took their love away. I don't want to become bitter or hurt anyone with my harsh words. Help Greg to understand what I'm feeling. Help him realize how intense the pain can be. I need Greg to help me through this time. Lord, I need You to help me too.''

I kept walking toward the end of the road, kicking stones from my path as I moved along. Suddenly I felt as though the Lord put His hand on my shoulder. I stopped and listened. The large green field of wheat that surrounded me swayed in the cool evening breeze.

Gently breaking into this stillness was the quiet thought, ''If I can set the stars in the sky, calm the sea, and stop the wind, surely I can direct your life.'' I clung to that thought and suddenly felt strong and sure. Whatever the future might hold, God would be with me. He had always been with me and always would be. Turning around to walk home, I felt like a new person. I felt as if I had touched the hem of Jesus' garment.

— *Chapter 12* —

A Visitation

God is our refuge and strength, a very present help in trouble.

Psalm 46:1

Leisurely walks alone at sunset became a habit for me as I reflected on the events of the recent past. I needed to give reasons for my emotions. Having recently made public my exit from the Church of Jesus Christ of Latter-day Saints, there were still conflicts, doubts, and a range of emotions to work through. Leaving the Mormon Church is not done in a moment. It is a process that requires time, effort, and a change of commitment.

One night after my evening walk and after the children were down for the night, Greg and I were enjoying our hour of Bible study and discussion. This nightly ritual had become a source of comfort and growth as we shared the things of God.

I followed along in my Bible as Greg read aloud from the Gospel of John. Suddenly he stopped in midsentence and looked at me with eyes that communicated love for me but at the same time something more. Surprised by his silence, I looked up to see tears in his eyes. I had known that he had been keeping from me some unpleasant situation in his company. He had been trying to protect me from another major problem that affected all of us.

His struggle at work was largely a struggle with his brother and partner in the business, Patrick. Because Patrick was not a Christian, nor did he want anything to do with Christianity, Greg was burdened for Pat. Concerned for his brother, Greg took time at work to talk to him about the claims of Christ. This discussion had gone on for weeks, consuming hours and energy which would otherwise have been spent on the business.

At the close of reading the Gospel of John one night, Greg began to pray: "God, I need You to show me what to do. I can't figure out any solution to this situation. I care about Pat, but I can't seem to reach him. The business is suffering, but Pat is more important. And I can't deal with all the tension and stress at work any longer. God, please show me."

As Greg prayed, I remembered: "If I can set the stars in the sky, calm the sea, and stop the wind, surely I can direct your life." Once again I experienced a surge of strength and comfort. Although I didn't have a solution for Greg, I did offer the reassurance that I was standing with him. Even with God's promise to be with us, we felt the responsibilities toward our business and toward Patrick weighing heavily on our hearts and minds.

Two weeks later, after much thought and many prayers, it was necessary to ask Patrick to leave the business. This lasted only a month. Having wrestled with his feelings and pressure from his brother to reconsider his decision, Greg rehired him. At first Greg felt that he was right in giving Pat a second chance. At the same time, he hoped that the debating would cease. It did not.

As Patrick resumed his responsibilities, the debating became more frequent and more heated than before. He had become deeply involved in New Age spiritual activity, and he was convinced that Greg was the one who was confused. Once again, but now with more anger and greater disappointment in his brother, Greg fired him permanently.

By mid-1981 the construction industry throughout the nation was becoming unstable. Federal funding was declining while interest rates were climbing, and our company was barely surviving. After heroic attempts to keep our employees working, Greg and I soon realized the inevitable: We would have to close the doors of the business.

We had started the company and had watched it grow from a three-man operation to a flourishing corporation. Now it seemed as if we were having to plan for its burial.

Over breakfast one morning, Greg somberly presented the legal steps of ending the company. We sat dejected and numb from the recent events as we totaled the debts of the company and faced unemployment. This financial reversal had happened in just a few short months.

As I drove into the driveway one October afternoon, I stopped to check the mailbox for the usual bundle of mail wrapped with a rubber band. Once inside the house, I began glancing at the envelopes. My heart sank as I read "Attorney-at-Law" on the return address of one envelope. There could be only one reason to be hearing from an attorney—my former husband, Ronny.

Not really wanting to know the contents of the letter, I tossed it aside and slowly read each of the other pieces of mail. Finally, having nothing else to read, it was time to open the letter. I had spoken with Ronny just once in the three years since our divorce. He had moved to another state once the settlement was final, and now I didn't want him intruding again. I prayed for strength as I opened the white envelope.

My hands trembled as I unfolded the neatly sealed piece of paper, and my fears were confirmed. I was being summoned to court for a hearing on child visitation rights. Ronny had not communicated with his children in years. Now, out of nowhere, he was back and demanding full visitation privileges.

I was angry. I resented Ronny's intrusion into our life and his sudden interest in children he didn't even know. And I was fearful of what this summons might mean to Benjamin and Brandon. Nightmarish memories crowded my mind.

When Greg returned home, I handed him the letter from the attorney. After he read it, we sat in silence for several minutes. Then, still without saying a word, he walked into the bedroom and shut the door behind him. He had loved the two boys as his own. He had fed them and changed their diapers. He had taught them to walk and to talk. He had loved them when they were unlovable and had comforted them when they were hurt. They had shared hunting and fishing trips. They had become friends. Suddenly, from nowhere, came the man who had abused them and left scars on their young minds and emotions, and he was demanding time with them.

As the day for the court hearing approached, Greg and I relied on strength from God. We clung to each other and shared tears and hugs whenever the subject came up, giving reassurance that all would be fine. At the hearing Ronny was awarded regular visitation rights. Now Greg and I prepared the children for the first visit.

The night before Benjamin and Brandon were to go with Ronny was a night of anxiety and dread. Would the boys be able to cope with the events of the next day? Would they come home safe and unharmed? Would they come home at all? After dinner Greg and I gathered all of the children around us and prayed. Each member of the family prayed. Only then were we able to sleep.

Benjamin and Brandon left with Ronny the next morning, and the Lord helped us through the long day. When they returned, we were relieved to see that they were safe. Although Brandon needed stitches where he had bumped his head while playing, that was the only incident. I thanked God for protecting Benjamin and Brandon and for comforting us while they were gone.

With the closing of our company, it became necessary to put our house up for sale and become renters. To our surprise and relief it sold quickly. Along with the bad news was some good news: There was going to be an addition to the family. We were anticipating the future with hope and high expectations.

— *Chapter 13* —

Spiritual Warfare

Go ye therefore and teach all nations, baptizing them in the name of the Father, and of the Son, and of the Holy Ghost.

Matthew 28:19

In the sixth month of my pregnancy the light of joyful anticipation dimmed. I became seriously ill and was confined to my bed, where I would slip in and out of consciousness. The days grew long as doctors could not find a reason for my illness. My perpetual nausea was accompanied by dizziness and fainting spells.

Greg, already restless about his continuing unemployment, now worried about me and all the unanswered questions surrounding my health. Soon I was sleeping for hours. I was oblivious to anything around me as I struggled with extended periods of unconsciousness.

Greg had spoken with the receptionist on the telephone just moments earlier. Now he carefully laid me in the back seat of the car and we raced to the doctor's office. My condition had become critical, the pain unbearable.

I lay on the examination table as if I had been drugged.

My feet rested in the cold metal stirrups, my arms were limp at my side, and my body burned with fever. Then, from the other end of the cloth which hung over the lower part of my body, came a whisper, "Your baby has died." I was conscious enough to hear the agonizing words, and tears began streaming down my face.

Despite the ordeal, I found support once again in my husband. As he gripped my hand while I was entering the hospital, I was overwhelmed with love for Greg and wanted to tell him so, but these last moments of consciousness faded into a sleep that lasted many hours.

Surgery was immediately performed to remove our baby, who had died from unknown causes several weeks earlier. Rather than rejecting it naturally, my body had held it tightly within my womb. The poisons from the lifeless baby had moved throughout my entire system, deadening senses as they spread.

While I was recovering, our prospects for employment were getting better. Greg was hired as a building superintendent, and his employment helped our family regain a degree of normality. And communication with my family seemed to be improving and becoming more frequent as my mother would call to share family news. Any mention of Jesus Christ, church involvement, or religion in general was off-limits. Still, I was thankful to know how my brother and sisters and their children were doing.

It was also gratifying to know that others in the family seemed to be trying to rebuild our broken relationship. But sometimes an anti-Mormon scare at the LDS Church would cool the relationship. When the storm passed, my family would again be open to me.

Greg and I were still attending Grace Community Church in Tempe, and we had met many special people during their hours of service to us while I was ill. Some church members had prepared meals for Greg and the children. Others had graciously cared for our children during the day, and others had cleaned our home. The congregation had been a family to us in our hour of need.

As the weeks passed, Greg and I saved enough money for a down payment on a new home. In April of 1982, my parents helped us purchase a large brick colonial house just before it went into foreclosure. At the end of the street stood another large brick home with white lacy curtains in the windows and a yard which was an irresistible playground for our children. It was my parents' new home.

Greg and I bought this house for several reasons. First, I hoped that being close to my family would help restore our relationship. I hoped to let them know by my actions that I loved them. I wanted to show them that I cared by occasionally leaving a meal or a batch of cookies at their house. And second, Greg and I were in a hurry to buy a house. We didn't want to be renters, and this house, on the verge of foreclosure, was a wise investment. We were excited to be packing our belongings and moving them to a new house.

It wasn't long after we had moved into the new neighborhood that Greg and I became aware of a disturbing situation: We had moved into the heart of a Mormon subdivision. The only other non-Mormon family had their house up for sale, planning to move when it sold. Greg and I realized immediately that the neighborhood could easily become a battleground for our children as well as for the two of us as the Saints learned of our participation with anti-Mormon groups.

We were more concerned for our children than ourselves. We wanted to protect them from any cruelty or isolation practiced by the other children. But because we had bought the house, we would remain and arm ourselves for whatever spiritual warfare we might face. We would trust God for His protection and His guidance.

Greg and I were also trusting God for His safekeeping in a new opportunity for ministry to help Mormons realize the deception of their religion and to follow Christ. This ministry began with a trip to California.

The morning we were to leave dawned bright and sunny. There wasn't a cloud in the sky, and the clean, crisp air was filled with the aroma of orange blossoms and honeysuckle. We had looked forward to this moment, and now we raced around the house taking care of last-minute details. The children were already staying with some Christian friends, and I called each one to reassure them that Daddy and I would return in just three days.

Then I closed the suitcase and reviewed my mental checklist one more time. We needed clothes for a three-day stay, and on this trip to California in late June this meant including bathing suits, beach towels, and suntan lotion. Greg and I were eager to be on our way to Burbank, traveling with our friends from Concerned Christians, Jim and Judy Robertson. The purpose of the trip was to appear in the investigative documentary film *The God Makers,* which was to be an exposé of Mormonism.

Believing in the purpose of the film, Greg and I were thrilled to have been asked to share with Mormons and with friends of Mormons the story of our journey to faith in Jesus Christ.

The Church of Jesus Christ of Latter-day Saints has borrowed the Judeo-Christian vocabulary and used it to cover up its pagan mysteries, doctrine, and practices. The vocabulary so familiar to Christians is merely a veil over basic Hindu and pagan mysticism, and it is a veil which cloaks the false teachings with a sense of innocence and purity.

Jeremiah Films was taking a bold step in producing this hard-hitting, investigative documentary on the theology and secrets of Mormonism. *The God Makers* would reveal the truth behind the carefully groomed facade that Mormonism displays to the outside world, a truth so bizarre that even most Mormons have trouble believing it when it is presented.

As we drove, I reviewed my life as a Mormon. Born

into a Mormon home, I had been ushered into Mormonism quite innocently. I had been involved in Sunday school and Primary, the afterschool church activities and training in doctrine. I had attended all the church's functions at the side of either my mother or my father. Even when I was young, the Mormon Church had been the nucleus of my existence. It had run through every vein and artery of my body.

At the age of 12, I advanced to Mutual, the young-adult meeting held once a week for personal growth and further education in Mormonism. Without Greg, I wouldn't have known anything other than Mormonism. In high school Greg had used Bible verses that spoke of the fact that I could be assured of my salvation from sin and that a new life in Christ had begun. He told me again and again that a life dedicated to Christ was the only path to peace and fulfillment.

The day to begin filming dawned hot and muggy, but the weather didn't lessen our enthusiasm for the task at hand. I had been too excited to have breakfast, and there were butterflies in my stomach. As we parked the car we heard an enthusiastic "Welcome to California!" We turned around as the tall, suntanned man finished his introduction. "My name is Pat and this is my beautiful new bride, Caryl Matrisciana."

Together we walked to the house. Pat led us into a cozy garden room filled with hanging plants. We all sat down on the large sectional and began to share details about our association with the Mormon Church. I explained that a Mormon stake president had advised me to divorce Greg because he was not a member of the Mormon Church. Blindly obeying this instruction, I suffered the heartache and pain of a divorce I didn't want and a marriage that was a mistake.

Jim and Judy had a similar story to tell. A Mormon bishop had advised Judy to divorce Jim because he had learned the truth about Mormonism. Although he had been a faithful LDS member for years, Jim discovered that Mormonism is not a Christian religion. He characterized it as "a deceitful work of Satan that imitates Christianity and leads people to eternal death rather than eternal life." Jim's faithful prayers for Judy were answered when she too came to understand the fallacies of Mormonism. She turned to the one and only God of the Bible, and she remained true to her marriage.

Now the scene was set and the lights were perfectly arranged. Caryl attended to our makeup, dress, and posture. "Silence. Scene One. Take One." The filming had begun. Greg and I were first. Drops of perspiration were frequently dabbed from our foreheads as we sat under the hot lights and shared our story. There were agonizing moments of reliving the pain and sorrow of Satan's intrusion in our lives. Pat, the producer of the film, vividly captured our sense of betrayal and the inner turmoil which resulted. By the end of the filming, the four of us were drained, but we were confident that God would bless our efforts and use the film to reach people with the good news of salvation through His Son, Jesus Christ.

Our drive home to Arizona was relaxing and encouraging as we shared our impressions of the trip and our thoughts about the film. Each had been touched in a different way. We shared a renewed appreciation for the purpose of our lives. We were here to proclaim the truth of Jesus Christ. As we had done this in front of the cameras, we had been blessed by the power of the Holy Spirit. We experienced the calm assurance that we were doing God's will by working on the film. It was right for us to warn other people of the trap of Mormonism. But while we were confident of our testimony, we were still vulnerable to temptation.

— Chapter 14 —

A Winter Chill

In God have I put my trust; I will not be afraid what
man can do unto me.

Psalm 56:11

Our return to Arizona after the spiritual refreshment
of the trip to California was a return to the battleground.
There was conflict in the neighborhood. Our children were
the brunt of fights and name-calling. Neighboring children
threw rocks into our yard, and several of our bicycles
disappeared. While the other children walked together
to and from the school bus stop, ours walked alone.
They knew the reason they weren't accepted was because
they weren't Mormon.

Greg and I were the objects of organized shunning by
the neighborhood. The woman I had always visited with
when we were gardening in our yards never spoke to me
after I returned from California.

With Greg working long hours in the construction industry and the four boys attending school, I had more
free time than ever before. So to my domestic responsibilities and church activities, I added several classes at

school. This ambitious schedule made the autumn months fly by.

Christmas 1983 was soon upon us. This meant Christmas carols in the air, Christmas cookies in the oven, and final exams for the head baker. With all this going on, I felt myself becoming more and more tired as the days slipped through my fingers. The cleaning, the cooking, the studying, and the raising of five active children comprised an endless job. My emotions and energy were being depleted, and I knew that something was bound to snap.

When Christmas Day arrived, it was one of the most beautiful I have ever known. We woke to the smell of a roasting turkey, which I had placed in the oven the night before. The tree's blinking lights cast multicolored hues around the room. Amid the wrapping paper, ribbons, and bows were five giggling and jubilant little people who were thrilled with their Christmas treasures.

When the early-morning excitement had passed, we decided to ride our new bicycles around the neighborhood. I buckled Jennifer into the infant seat and was ready for the bike ride. The air was cool, crisp, and invigorating. The wind made our noses and cheeks tingle as we briskly peddled around the neighborhood. As we rode, I suggested that we visit my parents. I motioned to Greg and the boys to follow me as I turned and headed for their home.

It had been months since Greg and I had communicated with my family, and now, on Christmas Day, I longed to be near them. I was beginning to accept the fact that I was no longer a part of their day-to-day life, yet the arrival of the holidays had reopened the wound. I spent many hours pleading with God to soften those hearts which were hardened against Greg and myself. And I prayed that they would also accept the gift of salvation, Jesus Christ.

My mother answered the door when I knocked.

Somewhat preoccupied, she quickly invited us in out of the cold. Immediately I sensed that she had something other than "Merry Christmas" on her mind. Her voice had a stiffness that I had come to recognize over the years as a sign that she was annoyed or upset. I noticed, too, that her hugs for each of the children and then for me were cold and forced. The slight squeeze was not followed by the standard peck on the cheek. And Greg received only the barest of acknowledgments.

My father sat in stony silence watching the sports channel on television. His feet rested on a small needle-point footstool, and his arms were firmly folded across his chest. His attention was focused entirely on the man in the football jersey who was racing downfield toward the goalpost.

Mother didn't offer us a seat, as was her custom. Instead, she remained standing just inside the doorway while she quietly asked the children if Santa had been good to them. She was quick and short as she responded to their answers. Her obvious uneasiness and the tense atmosphere began to worry me. It seemed clear that she was hiding something. As soon as I opened my mouth to talk, she leaned over to me and whispered harshly, "Don't think we don't know why you went to California! We know you were in that film!"

I opened my mouth to reply, but she wouldn't let me talk. "And your father and I never want to speak to you about it. We are just sick about the whole thing."

Having said that, she once again hugged each of us and opened the door. Greg and I walked out, chilled by the conversation and hug. The momentary confusion of the kids running for their bikes distracted us and eased the tension of the moment.

This was Christmas Day, the day set aside to celebrate the birth of Christ, to worship and adore Him, and to show love and goodwill to one another. My parents had not acknowledged the birth of Jesus Christ, nor had they shown goodwill toward their own relatives.

I prayed for the opportunity to share with my parents the hope I found in Jesus Christ. I wanted to tell them that because He loves me, He had taken my sins upon Himself and died in my place. I wanted to tell my parents that the church to which they had dedicated their lives was not the true church. I could acknowledge that the church offers an admirable set of morals and standards by which to live, but I needed to show my parents that the Mormon Church fails miserably to be Christian.

My mother and my father needed to realize that the Mormon Church teaches false doctrine that completely contradicts the Bible. Good works and self-righteous behavior cannot save anyone. There is only one way to be saved—and that way is Jesus Christ. Ephesians 2:8,9 was a passage they needed to hear and understand: "By grace are ye saved, through faith, and that not of yourselves: it is the gift of God—not of works, lest any man should boast."

Even though I heeded my mother's warning and didn't mention the film to my father, their friends and neighbors did. It wasn't long before they knew all the details except why I had appeared in the movie. To help them understand why I did it without mentioning the movie, I wrote a letter to them and shared details of my salvation, my love for Jesus, and my commitment to Him. Though I never received a reply, the message should have been clear.

As the weeks passed and winter melted into spring, my family's animosity grew more intense. Living on the same street with my parents was too close under these conditions. In March Greg and I sold our home and moved to Tempe, a move which put us closer to our church, Grace Community Church. We knew that there we would find solace in the love of good Christian friends and a pastor who deeply cared for us. We didn't know at the time that we were about to face the most frightening spiritual battle of our lives.

— *Chapter 15* —

An Ill Wind

My friends scorn me, but mine eye poureth out tears unto God.

Job 16:20

Our move to Tempe seemed right. There were many little signs of confirmation following our decision that gave us confidence that it was the right thing to do. We found a small house that exactly fit our requirements—a fixer-upper. Part of the house needed remodeling, just the kind of project Greg and I enjoyed. And this would give us the chance to work together, something we felt our relationship needed.

Now we would be located right across the street from our church, Grace Community Church. No more 45-minute drives to church; the children could now attend the many activities that were impossible to attend before. Greg and I would also be able to participate more in the life of the church. Indeed, the future did seem promising.

With the birth of our sixth child, Michael, in August of 1983, we realized that this home we enjoyed so much was too small for our family. After all, we had to accommodate two adults and six growing children. Although we were less than excited about moving again, the needs of the family were paramount.

Greg and I began to pray and search for a home large enough to accommodate our family, yet within our budget. We prayed regularly, eager to see how God would take care of us this time.

During this time another young couple came into our lives, Russ and Cindy. They were new members in our Sunday school class at Grace Community, and the four of us quickly became best friends. Part of this friendship was based on similar backgrounds that Cindy and I shared. Like me, Cindy had been born into a Mormon family, but had also accepted Jesus Christ as her Lord and Savior a few years earlier.

Cindy's friendship was a great joy and comfort to me. She was someone with whom I could identify because of similar experiences, someone with whom I could share the problems of exiting from Mormonism, particularly as it pertained to family relationships. Cindy and I could give each other support during the many times of depression and conflict that one feels after leaving the LDS Church. She became like a sister to me, since my sisters had closed me off from their lives. Russ and Cindy's friendship soon began to fill the places in my heart which had been left empty when my family had rejected me. They were a source of strength and encouragement.

The story of Cindy's conversion was an encouragement to us as we began witnessing to Mormons. The change in her life made us more dedicated in our ministry for Christ. Wherever the film *The God Makers* was shown in churches and Sunday school classes, we would be there to witness to its truth and answer questions. Our desire was to testify of Jesus Christ's salvation through faith and not of works, and in doing so to reach the lost for Him, particularly those in Mormonism.

Soon God provided the home we had trusted Him for.

We were enjoying a Sunday afternoon drive in early March. Hints of springtime were all around us as we drove through a section of homes we had always admired from a distance. The fruit trees and horse stables gave the neighborhood a warm country feeling. Because homes in this area didn't come up for sale often, we were excited when suddenly we noticed a small red sign—For Sale By Owner. After reaching an agreement with the owners, we bought the house. Greg and I rejoiced because God had made this purchase possible. There were too many evidences of His intervention and guidance to deny it. And in only two weeks we would be taking possession of it!

One morning the phone rang as I was packing some of our belongings in preparation for the move. It was the church secretary. "The pastor wants to meet with you and Greg as soon as possible. Could we arrange a time for the meeting?" she asked.

Greg and I returned home from our 4:00 o'clock meeting around 6:30, and I collapsed exhausted onto the huge living room chair. For two hours Greg and I had tried to untangle a serious misunderstanding with Russ and Cindy. We had tried to ease the hurt that resulted when Greg and I realized that a business partnership with Russ could not continue. When we made that decision, we wanted to protect and maintain our friendship, but our mutual efforts had failed.

The four of us left the pastor's study with a vow to remain friends, and our commitment had been sealed with tears and hugs. But the disagreement had not been mediated, and many questions remained. Would our friendship continue? Could the healing of our damaged relationship occur? And why were my emotions toward Cindy in such a conflict between love and hate?

As I sat in the chair I felt numb with disbelief. Greg sat across from me on the sofa, staring blankly ahead. At the same time I realized we had to take charge of our attitude concerning the problem in our relationship with

Russ and Cindy and work toward reconciliation.

The early Christian church grew because people were attracted to the Christians' love for one another, and we desired the same. We did not want to compromise our witness for Christ, both among believers and among our Mormon friends and family. The solution could only be found in being obedient to God's Word.

During this conflict I struggled with the temptation of an easy escape. Maybe it was Satan whispering words of comfort and advice: "Go back to your family. Go back to the Mormon Church. Those people will love you. Go back, Jolene. Go back." These chilling thoughts made me shudder, and I seemed to sense the heavens rumble as the beautiful serpent tried to make me believe his lie.

One of the things that made any resolution to our conflict difficult was that Cindy and I had been raised in a Mormon culture, and we brought to this experience some of those lifelong attitudes that were inbred by training and experience. Between Mormons, if one person is offended by another, asking forgiveness for one's offense is not enough. Extraordinary acts of kindness over a prolonged period is the only resolution. And this was one of our barriers to ending the conflict.

Days passed, but my spiritual battle continued. Greg and I continued going to church and to Sunday school, but our friendship with Cindy and Russ remained on hold. When we walked by each other on Sunday mornings, we couldn't get past the icy "hellos." As my feelings of rejection mounted, I enjoyed a corresponding increase in my sense of self-pity, a feeling that can only be resolved by forgiveness.

Two weeks earlier we had moved into our new home, and all my energies had been directed at making Greg and the children feel settled. Now we had time to spend in the yard, clipping shrubs, planting rosebushes, and trimming trees. Our fruit trees were loaded with peaches, apricots, and plums, and this meant afternoon snacks for the family as we sat outside under the trees and nibbled on these summer treats. We laughed as we stuffed our mouths full and then had pit-spitting contests. The kids giggled as Greg and I relaxed and became one of them.

Those two weeks organizing our new home and all of us working and playing together were gone all too quickly. Once again we were settled into a routine. Greg's hours at work were long and strenuous. The children were busy with their summer activities. And I was left alone with my thoughts, "Those Christians don't accept you, Jolene. You just don't fit in. You're different, and you're awkward when you try to belong. No one really cares about you. You are alone, Jolene. Alone."

Beginning to believe these lies brought on by my own insecurities, I walked around the house in a bewildered daze and spent hours sitting on the bed staring out the window. Why in the midst of all of the beauty that God had created did I feel so despondent? Where was my self-confidence? In its place I felt self-pity and unworthiness.

I also spent a lot of time wondering about truth. I knew too well the trauma that comes to a person when he realizes that what he had longed believed to be true is in fact false. That had been my experience, and I had seen other people face it. I had seen the falsity of Mormonism when I had studied the Bible and accepted its message —that is, that Christ Jesus came into the world to save sinners (1 Timothy 1:15). I had seen other people, though, admit to the false teachings of Mormonisn and yet be unable to accept the truth of salvation through Jesus Christ. They usually emerged from their indoctrination with the conviction that if Mormonisn is not true, then there must not be any truth.

But I *did* know the truth. I knew Jesus Christ, and He had consoled me in my hour of need. But now I wasn't experiencing the peace I had known before. More than ever I needed the reassurance that only Jesus can give.

My grieving took my eyes off Jesus Christ and turned them inward. Instead of following Him, I began to follow my own direction.

Despite this grief and seeming separation from God, I tried not to have second thoughts about my decision to leave Mormonism. I tried to cling to Jesus Christ as I sensed that the powers of darkness stood ready to descend on me. If I let them invade my thoughts, they could take control. But the invasion had already begun.

— Chapter 16 —

A Relapse

Watch and pray that ye enter not into temptation; the spirit indeed is willing, but the flesh is weak.

Matthew 26:41

It was a warm evening in early summer in Tempe. Greg and I were preparing to attend another showing of *The God Makers* at a local church. Still trying to reconcile the broken friendship with Russ and Cindy, I mustered my strength to pick up my purse and my Bible and walk with Greg to the car.

The evening began with a short introduction of the film, followed by a testimony by a former Mormon who had given his life to Jesus Christ. Prior to the showing, Greg and I were introduced as people whose story was told in the film.

Sometime during the film I became aware of oppression that I believed to be demonic. It seemed to be saying to me, "Maybe this film is just a little too harsh, Jolene. After all, they are good people." As I listened, the voice continued, "Maybe you should go back to the Mormon Church and make sure that the accusations in the film are valid." By the end of the film I was fidgeting nervously. Again the voice spoke. "What will it hurt? You could go back just once. Surely that wouldn't be wrong."

The words and impression were so strong that when the lights went on I looked around for the "imp" who had seemed to be sitting on my lap during the film. It was nowhere to be seen, and I breathed deeply and folded my hands in my lap. They were cold, and I was feeling nauseous. I wanted to leave immediately, but it was too late. People were already gathering around us to ask questions, and the answers were not forthcoming. I just stood there and let Greg lead the conversation. With a few quick and questioning glances at me, he knew that something was wrong. He politely dismissed us, grabbed my arm firmly, and walked me to the car.

"What's wrong, Jolene? You're white as a ghost!" he said once we were alone in the parking lot.

"I don't know. I think I'm going to be sick. I had the weirdest sensation during the film. It was as if someone was talking to me and telling me not to watch the film anymore."

"I wasn't going to say anything unless you did first, but I have noticed a heavy oppression around our home, Jolene, and it frightens me. It should frighten you, too." We drove home in silence.

That night I lay awake in bed while Greg slept. I felt myself wrestling once again with the voice that said, "Go home. Go back to the Mormon world where you belong. Give up your church. Give up those Christians who hurt you. Give up." I found myself longing for the peace, the control, the security of my Mormon childhood. I wanted the easy path of acting on decisions that other people made for me. In my struggle I cried out, "But the Mormons don't have Jesus!" This time there wasn't a response. I waited but the voice didn't answer my cry.

I threw back the bedcovers and went into the bathroom.

As I stood there, staring at myself in the mirror, I felt ashamed of participating in the conversations instead of cutting them off. How could I have listened to Satan's promptings? How could I have paid attention to his whisperings? My strength gave way, and I slid to the floor and sobbed, not knowing what to do. I was slowly succumbing to this unwanted power, and it was taking control of my thought processes and interfering with my relationship with God.

Life had recently been an adventure with God—growing, sharing, and serving Him. Now wild feelings that didn't make sense, and unpredictable reactions to the events of life, kept interfering with my days. Relying only on my emotions kept me from serving the God I loved. When I was able to stand strong against this demonic influence, the power seemed to return later with seven times the strength. Right now I was overwhelmed and defenseless.

Two days after this horrible night, I received a phone call from my mother. She wanted to tell me that Ellen had had a baby boy. (Because Ellen already had four girls, a boy was cause for celebration.) On one level of communication she informed me that I had missed the celebration of this fifth child and long-awaited son. But on a more subtle level she made her disappointment clear that I hadn't participated in this important family event.

"Why do you have to separate yourself from the rest of us?" When I didn't respond, she kept talking. "Even your cousin, Debbie, has finally joined the church. She's almost ready to go to the temple with her husband."

After a period of silence, I finally managed to say, "I know."

"Next week," my mother continued, "Sandra and her husband are going to speak at a sacrament meeting. It would be nice if you came and showed her you care."

My mother was finished. She had said what she had

wanted to say, and had communicated even more. Discouraged, I hung up the phone and sat at the kitchen table weak and with feelings of inadequacy. Now Satan was adding to these feelings a layer of guilt.

As I looked at my life, I felt as though I had missed the mark. Greg and I had set high ideals for our family life. Our desire for ourselves and our children was that we would think and behave as true Christians—that biblical principles would rule our lives. Now Satan seemed to be telling me I had failed as a mother, a wife, and a friend. When he reminded me of all the programs the Mormon Church offers for family growth and for personal development, programs my church did not have, I found myself yearning for the "better way of living" that the Mormon Church promised.

This was all the inertia I needed to make up my mind. I was going to attend the sacrament meeting and listen to my sister and brother-in-law as they shared their testimonies with the congregation. This was a special opportunity that every Mormon would cherish, and I wanted Sandra to know that I did love her by my attendance.

On Sunday morning, June 24, I was up and dressed before anyone else. We weren't to be at the ward until 2:00 in the afternoon, so we took time to visit my parents. It was an opportunity to tell them in person that we would be at the sacrament meeting. This would be my first step back inside an LDS Church in over six years.

When we stopped at my parents' house, my father invited us in. He explained that Mother was at a Relief Society meeting and would return just in time to go to Sandra's ward. I replied that we would also be going to the meeting to hear her speak, and I asked if he and my mother would save a place for our family to sit with them. "Of course we will," was all he said.

It was exactly 2:00 when we entered the parking lot of my sister's ward. By now my eagerness to attend the

meeting had become a good case of nerves. I was glad
that Greg, who had fought the idea all along, was walking
beside me and holding my hand. The children walked
behind us.

As we sat down next to my mother, I looked around.
The building was just what I had expected, the same as
it had been when I was a child. The large room was starkly
furnished with plain wooden pews. The bishop, his two
counselors, Sandra, her husband, and the afternoon's
third speaker sat in front. The meeting would follow the
familiar program, with the focus on the speakers and
some music.

During the opening prayer, the first song, and the
announcements, the sacrament of communion was
prepared. Now it was time to receive the bread and water
elements. (Mormons believe that the new wine which
Christ drank was not fermented. They therefore use water
in their sacrament and avoid any chance for the grape
juice to ferment and become wine.) Twelve-year-old boys
(deacons in their Aaronic priesthood) passed the elements
to the congregation. As the container of bread was passed
down our pew, I remembered the years of my childhood.
To those in the LDS Church, the act of taking communion
represented a commitment to the principles of Jesus rather
than remembering the ultimate sacrifice that Jesus paid
with His death on Calvary for our sins.

When a member of the ward did not partake of the
bread and water, my friends and I knew that the person
was not worthy in some way. We would have fun guessing
why Brother or Sister So-and-So had not taken the
elements. Now I would be the one not participating. I
sensed the eyes of curious onlookers on me, and slowly
sank in my seat. I had had my name removed from the
church records some five years earlier, and I was no longer
eligible to partake of this Mormon sacrament.

Soon it was Sandra's turn to speak. I felt guilty as I
rather unexpectedly enjoyed her talk. The longer I

listened, the easier it was for me to be there. She talked about the special relationship she had with her husband and about her thankfulness for the Mormon Church. After she closed her talk, her husband took his place at the microphone. As he spoke, more memories from my childhood flooded my mind, and I realized how much I missed those times that I had shared with my family.

When we left the meeting that afternoon, I was frightened that I had enjoyed being in church—in the Mormon Church—with my parents, my sister, and her family. The familiar surrounding was comforting compared to what I had recently been through. Even the undisciplined children who (as always) were running through the halls did not annoy me. The afternoon had been a step back into time—a step back into a comfortable, safe time.

Lying in bed that night, I longed for a close relationship with my family. I wanted to be able to sit with them, relaxed and talking comfortably as we enjoyed each other's company. Was this a dream which would never happen? I didn't know, but I did hope that my presence at the meeting had been a step toward reconciliation.

However, the events of the day had caused some tension between Greg and me which we left unspoken. Neither of us wanted to approach the subject. We had exchanged glances all evening, each waiting for the other to speak first. At the end of the day we hadn't yet talked about the meeting, and the time still didn't seem right. With a quick kiss we said goodnight and fell asleep.

As the week progressed, I found the events of Sunday afternoon almost unbelievable—that I had attended a Mormon Church, and that Greg had gone with me. The afternoon also seemed unreal as I thought of how we had a good time with my family. Were things finally changing? Were they beginning to accept us? Or were we beginning to give in to their pressure? Were Greg and I the ones who were changing? Were Greg and I compromising our witness in order to improve our relationship with my

family? Would we have to sacrifice our beliefs in order
to be accepted by my family?

Just as Eve had been tempted by the serpent with a lie
in the Garden of Eden, it seemed that Greg and I were
now being tempted by the serpent with a lie. We were
tempted with the proposition that we would find friendship and love in the Mormon Church.

Satan knew that we had been disappointed and hurt
in our friendship with Russ and Cindy, and he knew that
I was still struggling over the loss of my family. Satan
also knew that Greg and I were weak and vulnerable. We
longed to be loved, and yet we were afraid of being hurt
again. We had therefore isolated ourselves from the Christian community (by not attending church or being among
believers) long enough for Satan to enter our world and
gently lead us into his trap.

Early Friday morning after the sacrament meeting, I
awakened suddenly. A comment of my mother came to
mind. As we walked out of the church on Sunday, I had
asked her if Jesus Christ was her personal Lord and Savior. She answered with a strong voice, "Yes, He is. I do
have a personal relationship with Jesus Christ." This
statement was perplexing because Mormons do not believe
in a "personal" relationship with Jesus Christ. So how
did my mother reconcile her statement with the LDS
teachings? Did she really believe that salvation was found
in Jesus alone?

For answers to my questions about this apparent
contradiction, I called my mother, an upstanding LDS
woman. "Mom, it's Jolene. Could you do something for
me?" Without waiting for a reply, I continued. "Could
you find out what ward I'm living in and the name of
the bishop of the ward? I want to have some Mormon
missionaries visit me here."

"Is that really what you want?" she asked after a short
pause.

"Yes—and the sooner the better," I answered. I was

anxious to know what the Mormon Church taught about a personal relationship with Jesus.

Shortly after talking to my mother, I received a call from Elder Craig. We scheduled an appointment for 7:00 the following evening. When Greg returned home from work, I told him my plan.

"You did what?" he demanded.

"I just want some answers," I began. "I'm tired of listening to everyone's opinions. I want to know the truth from the church itself. If they really don't want their members to have a personal relationship with Jesus, then it's all over. I will have the answer I need, and I won't ask any more questions. My mother, though, will need to know the truth."

Greg had always refused any type of personal confrontation with officials of the Mormon Church, especially in our home. I knew he was trying to be patient with me now as he considered what I had done and the possible consequences. After a long silence, Greg took a deep breath and uttered a quiet "Okay." Then he said no more.

Because the Church of Jesus Christ of Latter-day Saints continually changes its doctrine and practice because of "continued revelations," I thought I needed someone from the church to come and explain what it now stood for. For example, when I was young, members of the church were taught not to say they were Christian, but Mormon. Now, however, they are taught to refer to themselves as Christian. So all I wanted to do was ask the missionaries of the LDS church if the church now taught a personal relationship with Jesus Christ. And this was the beginning of an episode in our lives that got totally out of hand by the end of the next week.

— *Chapter 17* —

Playing With Fire

Beware of false prophets, which come to you in sheep's clothing, but inwardly they are ravening wolves.

Matthew 7:15

It was 7:00 P.M. sharp when the doorbell rang. I answered the door and was pleasantly greeted by two men in suits and white shirts.

"Hi, Mrs. Coe? We're from the Church of Jesus Christ of Latter-day Saints. I'm Elder Craig and this is my companion, Elder White. May we come in?" I knew immediately that the taller of the two, Elder Craig, was in charge. He would, no doubt, do most of the talking while Elder White agreed smilingly with everything he said.

I ushered the two missionaries into the family room, where they sat down on the sofa. Greg and I sat adjacent to them on the loveseat, and the older children sat quietly on the rug beside us observing it all. We all smiled and made small talk for the first few minutes. Then Greg spoke.

"Well, gentlemen," Greg began, "we are Christians,

we are members of Grace Community Church in Tempe, and we love the Lord very much. Jolene's family belongs to your church, and so we are fairly familiar with your doctrines and beliefs. Still, we do have a few questions which we would like you to answer for us.''

Again Elder Craig took charge in his confident, relaxed manner. "Well, that's why we're here. We want to answer any questions you have about our church. Let me suggest, though, that you give us the opportunity to share with you some presentations that are designed especially for people like you who want to know exactly what we Mormons believe. I'm sure that we will be able to answer all of your questions through these discussions. The illustrations we provide will help you gain a complete understanding of the Mormon Church.''

He seemed so sure that we would enjoy his presentations that Greg and I didn't know how to refuse his offer. Besides, Greg and I had heard a lot about these ''discussions,'' but we had never been exposed to them. Furthermore, it only seemed fair that we let the Mormons present their case before we refuted their arguments about preexistence and an eternal state of progression to godhood. Greg saw my nod of approval and agreed to meet with them on Monday night when they would bring their discussion material.

Greg and I decided not to make a big deal over these discussions, but we also decided not to tell anyone about the visits until our questions had been answered. Our visitors had been personable. They were sincere and easy to talk to, and we believed they would provide answers to our questions. We were eager to hear their discussions.

When the elders returned on Monday evening, they brought with them a large briefcase and several charts. Before beginning the first discussion, Elder Craig asked Greg if he would like to open with a prayer. Greg prayed, and the discussion began.

This time Elder White led the conversation and referred

often to the spiral-bound charts on his lap. Greg and I
saw that he knew his material well and that he spoke with
conviction concerning its truth. He began by reading the
phrase on his first chart: "The Church of Jesus Christ."

"You said you are members of Grace Community
Church in Tempe. Correct?" he asked.

Greg nodded.

"Well, as I'm sure you are aware, there are several
different churches on the earth today. Wouldn't you
agree, however, that despite the numerous churches
available, people are discouraged, confused, and looking
for something better in these troubled times of ours?
Many people are looking for the right church. They want
to avoid the churches that are wrong. In your opinion,
Mr. Coe, wouldn't it be important for God to give us
direction and help today as we look for the right church?"

"I'd rather not give my opinion yet. Please go on,"
Greg answered.

This response didn't seem to bother Elder White, and
he calmly continued his presentation as if Greg had given
just the answer he wanted. "Do you think that our
heavenly Father intended for this confusion to exist? No."
He turned to the next page and revealed a picture of Jesus.
"Many years ago there were prophets living on this earth.
We know this from the Bible, don't we? If you had lived
back then and had had a question about which church
was true, you would probably have gone to the prophets
for advice, right?" Elder White's question was directed
at me this time.

"Yes, I guess I would," I replied somewhat hesitantly.
I felt he knew I would give the answer he was wanting.

Very pleased with my response, Elder White continued.
"Yes, and the Lord did use His prophets to instruct people
and to relay His messages to them. The prophets were very
important to the Lord, weren't they?"

Together, Greg and I nodded yes.

The elder turned the page and went on. "What does this

knowledge of history suggest about the many conflicting doctrines taught in today's churches?''

Again Greg remained silent and motioned the elder to continue.

Elder White then explained that these conflicting doctrines point out our need for another prophet who can show us the right set of beliefs. He stressed how helpful it would be to have, in our own time, a prophet on earth who could be the mouthpiece of the Lord. He then moved forward to the edge of the couch.

"We are here tonight, Mr. and Mrs. Coe, to testify to you that the Lord did indeed call a man to be a prophet in this dispensation. His name was Joseph Smith. As a young man, Joseph Smith was confused about which denomination to join, and so he asked God for direction. He went into a grove of trees, knelt down, and began to pray.

"Suddenly, right before him, Joseph Smith saw a large pillar of light that seemed brighter than the sun. When this pillar descended, he saw two personages whose form was as men but whose brightness and glory defied all description. One of the figures spoke to Joseph Smith, calling him by name and pointing to the other: 'Joseph, this is my beloved Son. Hear Him.' With that, the other figure spoke. 'Joseph Smith, don't join any of those churches. All of them are wrong.' ''

Elder White turned the page of the flip-chart on his lap. "Who do you think these two personages were?"

I answered, "They're supposed to be God the Father and His Son, Jesus Christ."

"That's right!" Elder White's enthusiasm was somewhat humorous. He proceeded to explain that Joseph Smith's vision teaches us that God has a flesh-and-blood body, and that because Joseph Smith saw two personages, it was reasonable to believe that God the Father and Jesus Christ are two different beings.

Our Mormon visitor then turned to his next chart—

"Apostles and Prophets." Elder White explained that Joseph Smith was commanded to restore the true church, and then he had a question for us. "Since the church that Joseph Smith was commanded to restore is the church of Jesus Christ, do you feel that it should be administered by apostles and prophets today, as it was in ancient days?"

By now Greg's facial expressions were indicating extreme annoyance. I too was annoyed by this battery of leading questions. But I also didn't want to break the flow of Elder White's obviously memorized speech, so I nudged Greg to answer the question. Greg glanced at me as if to let me know that he was only going to be polite. He then answered, "It would seem reasonable."

Elder White smiled at Elder Craig. He probably thought that he was finally getting through to us. Now Greg was answering questions.

Elder White then asked Elder Craig to read Ephesians 2:19,20: "Now therefore ye are no more strangers and foreigners, but fellow citizens with the saints, and of the household of God, and are built upon the foundation of the apostles and prophets, Jesus Christ himself being the chief cornerstone."

Elder White again spoke. He told us that there has always been only one church—the church of Jesus Christ—but that at the time of Christ's death, the church experienced a time of apostasy or falling away. Eventually the apostles were killed, and God's word was no longer on this earth. As the last believers died, the church and the whole human race entered what is called the "Dark Ages."

The lesson continued: "In the 1800's, God found someone He could use to restore the only true church to the earth. The prophet was Joseph Smith and the church is the Church of Jesus Christ of Latter-day Saints. With Jesus Christ as its chief cornerstone, with the 12 apostles, and with a living prophet—three characteristics of the church in the days of Christ—this church must truly be *the* church of Jesus Christ.'' The case, in Elder White's view, was irrefutable.

Having finished the general history of the church, Elder White then gave his own personal testimony. He declared that all he had shared was true, and that it had been made known to him through a manifestation of the Holy Spirit. He declared that the prophet Joseph Smith was a true prophet of God and that the Book of Mormon was a true account of the people on the North American continent who lived at the time of Jesus.

Elder White then explained how Greg and I could come to know for ourselves the truth of the things he had taught. We needed only to pray with sincere hearts and genuine faith in God. If we did that, we would experience a burning in the chest near the heart. This sign would confirm the truthfulness of Elder White's teachings, and we would feel the steady assurance that every aspect of Mormonism is true.

Next, Elder Craig assured Greg and me that he too had this same testimony as to the truth of Mormonism. He could echo the experience and the faith that Elder White had described. Then both Elder Craig and Elder White thanked us for having them in our home. After shaking our hands, our Mormon guests left—but only after scheduling meetings for the subsequent four evenings.

Elder White and Elder Craig used those meetings to reinforce the teachings they had already presented. They discussed once again the Mormon view of Adam and Eve's fall. They reviewed Joseph Smith's life and the doctrines he had established as gospel—the plan of salvation through works and good deeds, the Thirteen Articles of Faith, the Word of Wisdom, the Book of Mormon, the church's Doctrine and Covenants, the Pearl of Great Price, and the principle of preexistence. Finally, the elders stressed again the importance of the family, tithing, genealogies, temples, and the ritual of baptism into the Mormon Church.

By the end of the week only one discussion remained, and we scheduled this final meeting for the following Tuesday. During this break between the Friday discussion and the Tuesday interview, however, Greg and I were numb. We felt as if we were being carried helplessly along on a swift current. And the rushing waters were taking us straight for the rapids of further involvement in the Mormon Church. At the time we felt wasted and uninvolved. We seemed unable to make a decision which would change the direction we were going. Our wills seemed to be in neutral, and we seemed rather detached from the reality of the disastrous course we were on.

The passage of time also seemed strange. Our visit to Sandra's sacrament meeting only 12 days earlier now seemed like a year ago. Since that Sunday our minds had entertained the strange doctrines and unanswered questions of the Mormon Church. My parents, Ellen, Sandra, and Jim had called almost daily since they learned of our discussions with the missionaries.

In addition to offering their prayers and support, members of my family began to visit our home. Their presence in our home and their close attention effectively kept Greg and me from spending any time with a Christian friend or our pastor. This attention and renewed love gave me great hope for a reconciliation with my family.

Still, interfering with these thoughts and hopes for a reconciliation with my family was the sense that I was being smothered by doctrines I did not believe. Greg and I were playing with fire—with dangerous and eternal fire—but I let my desire to once again be part of my family blind me to the potential consequences of our discussions with the missionaries. Furthermore, there was the nagging thought that maybe Greg and I had missed something about the Mormon Church in all our experience and research. I wondered whether they really did have the truth. I seriously considered the possibility that before now I just hadn't been able to see the truth of the Mormon Church.

Our minds were strangely fogged. Greg and I had learned that Christianity and Mormonism were very different; we had learned that they were thoroughly contradictory on such fundamental doctrines as salvation, the person of God, and the person of Jesus Christ. We had completely trusted the Bible as the authentic basis for our faith. Now, however, we were asking, "Could the Mormons really be right?" Perhaps the missionaries were correct in saying that the Bible needed to be made complete by the Book of Mormon, the Doctrine and Covenants, and the Pearl of Great Price. Perhaps the elders were correct in teaching that Joseph Smith and his church provided the only real means of salvation.

But much more convincing than doctrine was my own desire to be reunited with my family. My longing for this was so strong that I became willing to rejoin the Mormon Church, if that was the price. I reasoned that since I was a Christian and believed in the Christian doctrine as found in the Bible alone, I would be a Christian within the Mormon Church. I would not accept the Mormon belief—only their way of life. By now my reasoning was sounding convincing to Greg.

— *Chapter 18* —

Not Thy Will

Beloved, believe not every spirit, but try the spirits whether they are of God, because many false prophets are gone out into the world.

1 John 4:1

Saturday morning arrived, and Greg and I were free from caring for our five oldest children for the day. This left us with our youngest, the baby. We decided to visit the LDS temple, which was just a few minutes drive away from our home, and spend the day walking around the grounds and perhaps taking the guided tour or viewing their movies of the history, beliefs, and activities of the church.

Surrounded by the summertime beauty of colorful flowers and lush green landscaping, the temple was striking in its splendor. The towering palm trees that swayed in the gentle breeze of the warm day framed the temple, which had been patterned after King Solomon's. Carved marble walls showed early Mormon pioneer treks with women in bonnets, wagon trains pulled by oxen, and small children running alongside. The feeling of ancient history and opulence was unmistakable as we made our way to the visitors' center for a tour.

The tour itself offered more pictures of Mormon history and the Mormon lifestyle. Painted murals, animated talking statues, filmstrips, and a motion picture offered the Mormon perspective of life—past, present, and future. Once again the emphasis was on close family relationships and high moral standards—which made the church sound warm and inviting. We both noticed a strange feeling of peace and contentment as we continued past life-sized tapestries of tranquil scenes from the Mormon way of life.

Greg and I stayed at the temple until 9:00 in the evening. We had watched film after film present the different aspects of Mormonism, and we had strolled around the lighted temple grounds. As the day drew to a close, Greg and I found ourselves wondering if the magnificent walls of the temple had, as the Mormons claimed, really witnessed God. We wondered if Jesus had actually stood on the fibers of the soft carpet inside. We wondered if the temple was a necessary element of true worship of God. The presentation we had seen that day began to plant questions in our minds.

While we had these questions, at the same time we were certain of some basic doctrines plainly stated in the Bible. We knew that Christ's death on the cross was the only bridge between God and mankind. We knew that because of Christ's sacrificial death everyone can approach God without a priest or a temple (Hebrews 10:19-22). While we couldn't make that belief fit with the Mormon teaching, yet for some reason we didn't let this inconsistency cloud our wonderful day. As we drove home, a feeling of peace and contentment overshadowed any doctrinal question which had surfaced during the day.

When we arrived home, the first thing I did was to call my mother and share the news of our day's outing. Her quivering voice said that she was crying tears of joy. The feeling I had of being accepted by her, of doing something she approved, was delightful. This elation continued the next day, when she and my father drove us to their church. For the first time we rode together to the ward where Greg and I would soon become members.

The morning passed quickly. First there was the sacrament meeting, after which we were introduced to many of the members of the ward before being ushered into the adult classrooms by the bishop. After the class I went to the Women's Relief Society, the children went to primary, and Greg went to the men's priesthood meeting.

I was apprehensive about attending the Relief Society meeting, since I hadn't been to one in years. Then the president introduced my mother and me. If the women had not recognized my face, they surely recognized my name and realized that I was the one who had been leading people away from Mormonism and speaking against the church.

For the first time since Greg and I had started talking with the missionaries, I felt uneasy, insecure, and ashamed. I felt that something inside me, something very important, was slipping away. Was I letting God down? Was I abandoning the mission He had called me to? Was I denying the God who had seen me through so much? Although I knew but didn't want to admit that the answer to these questions was yes, I continued toward my goal of acceptance and love by family and toward friends whom I thought wouldn't let me down.

As I waited in the hallway for Greg after the Relief Society meeting, my attention was diverted by warm greetings from friends and strangers. Their kindness and sincerity eased the tension until I felt that strange calmness once again. The peace came just as it had before. And a voice seemed to say, "Don't worry about anything. Don't try to understand anything, Jolene. Just trust me, and you'll be happy."

On Tuesday evening I seemed to be following the advice of this voice. The missionaries and their supervisor from their missionary office arrived as scheduled. This final session was a rapid-fire review of all they had taught and explained in the past five meetings. Elders Craig and White carried the discussion, speaking for us as well.

Greg and I felt carried along by the tide of information and their encouragement to join the church. Unlike other decisions we had made together, we didn't think through the consequences of joining the Mormon Church. In retrospect, it seems that we were not thinking at all but had unknowingly reached a point where we chose to be influenced. Our usual practice was to consider the possible repercussions of any decision. But this time I don't remember thinking clearly or feeling anything. The evening is only a blur in my mind. I can only remember the hum of the elders' voices as I was sucked into Satan's deception.

Seeing the missionaries out the door after several hours of a one-sided discussion, Greg and I began planning to meet once again with them on Thursday evening. In two days we would be baptized into the Mormon Church. The usual preparation time for a baptism was several weeks, but for whatever reason we were judged ready to be baptized after only a few nights of discussion. This fast-moving pace of events kept Greg and me from realizing the seduction to which we were succumbing. We were now at the precipice, yet we didn't realize it. That subjective sense of peace kept us moving smoothly toward their goal of baptism for us. And that peace remained with us— until Thursday morning, July 12, 1984.

During that Saturday we spent at the temple, Greg mentioned several times the serenity and peace that came over him even though he recognized he was in hostile territory. He repeated several times how strangely at peace he felt and how he even enjoyed it. Whenever he would think for a moment about what he was doing he would

say to himself, "Oh, what am I doing here!" This would
be followed by the thought, "Just be happy and enjoy
yourself." I had that pleasant feeling too, but with me
it seemed more natural because I was in familiar surround-
ings that had played a positive role in my earlier years.

The next morning I awoke feeling extremely nervous
and emotionally wrung out. I was trying to calm myself in
a warm bubble bath. Suddenly Greg burst through the
door of my room pale as a ghost.

"I can't go through with this, Jolene. It just can't be
right. I need time. I'll be back later!" And with that he
grabbed his Bible and raced out of the house.

At first I was furious. How could he leave me alone
without discussing it? As the minutes passed, my anger
faded. I found myself wishing he would not return until
after the scheduled time of the baptism. But this gave me
a few hours alone to think.

The slam of the door as Greg left the house had seemed
to jar me back to reality—a reality I had left behind since
the missionaries had shared their first presentation with
us. I suddenly wondered why Greg and I had accepted
so easily everything that Elders Craig and White had
shared with us. Why had we so passively received their
doctrine and instruction? Why were the events moving
us so quickly?

The feeling was similar to what I had experienced during the events leading up to my marriage to Ronny. The
decision was made and the plans were set; it was too late to
change the course of things, and I followed through
without thinking. Once again, a decision seemed to be
made without me; other people were now directing my
life while I followed. Now I was having second thoughts.

I began to hope that Greg would not return in time for
us to go to the baptism. If he didn't come back, I wouldn't
go alone. But I did want to proceed with the baptism for
one important reason: I wanted to be accepted by my
family. In this tug-of-war between God and family, I

resigned myself to the idea that our problems would work themselves out, which was another way of not accepting responsibility for my decisions. That thought, however, did not provide a great deal of peace or comfort. I still hoped to find this involvement with the Mormon Church a bad dream.

Around noon Greg returned. He pulled me aside from my work and said, "Jolene, I'm going through with the baptism—but I'm only doing it for you. As I was driving, I began to pray. I asked God for some kind of peace about our decision. The peace didn't come, but I was given a vision. I was told that within ten years I would be a prophet of the Mormon Church and that I was to follow through with the baptism. The message promised that everything would be okay." He put his arms tightly around my shoulders and began to sob tears which seemed to be tears of guilt and remorse. His actions contradicted the words he had tried to say so confidently.

I wanted to look into his face but couldn't loosen his grip as he held me tight and continued to sob. Then, after several minutes, Greg said, "There was more to the vision, but I can't tell you right now."

He wiped the dampness from his face and sat down on the bed. "I don't understand this, Jolene. My heart is aching to be near God, but something seems to be in the way. As I said, I will go through with this, but I don't want to. If I do, maybe I can bring them to Jesus."

Later I realized that this was Greg's way of rationalizing his baptism. He was not baptized to convert Mormons to Christianity but to keep our family together. He recognized the strong pull of my family and how desperately I wanted to be restored to them. He also considered that if he weren't baptized, he might face the possibility of another divorce from me. Therefore he rationalized his baptism with the idea that he could be a missionary to the Mormons.

While he talked, I felt as though my body were being

twisted and wrung by some unknown but powerful force. At the time I was not fully aware of what was happening to us. I didn't understand the power we were battling. But there was an ambivalence on my part, even a weak desire to call the whole thing off—to cancel the baptism—to stay away from the Mormon stake building —but I couldn't find the strength or courage to act. Disappointing my family, my childhood friends, my new friends, and even those people I didn't know who would attend the baptism out of love and concern was too strong a desire. But instead of sharing this with Greg, I just sat silently beside him on the bed.

"Jolene, I don't want to do this! I'm not going to that temple, and I'm not going to be baptized! You can go if you want to, but I just can't!" Usually reserved, Greg was now very demonstrative as he paced back and forth on the living room carpet. Again he yelled to me, "I'm not going!"

My own nerves were raw. I stormed down the stairs. "Fine!" I yelled back. "Don't come with me! I don't care anymore! Just leave me alone!" And I ran back to our bedroom.

As I stared into the closet searching for clothes to wear to the baptism, I was saddened by having lashed out at Greg. He couldn't know that I was feeling the same conflicts as he was, but I was unable to tell him. So I walked downstairs to ask his forgiveness.

"Greg," I said, crying, "do you want me to call my dad and cancel the whole thing?"

"No. Jolene, I'm sorry. I told you that I'd go through this with you, and I will." With that I almost wished he had said yes.

It was nearly 4:00 in the afternoon and time to leave for the baptism. The kids were in the car waiting for Greg and me to join them. They had heard our yelling, but they hadn't asked any questions. I knew that they must be confused. After all, they knew we were joining the church whose false teachings we had been exposing for the past years. They had asked many questions during the past ten days, but when they realized we were going to avoid the topic, their questions stopped.

As we closed the front door of our home, Greg made one last attempt to change our plans. "Are you sure you want to go through with this?" he asked.

Instead of answering him, I glanced over at him and said, "Come on. We'll be late."

As we drove to the stake building where the baptism would take place, I silently cried to God. "Forgive me, God, but love me. Please forgive my weakness. I know I'm choosing to live the way the world teaches. I know You, God, and I know that I should be living for You as You instruct us. But I'm disobeying. Somehow, Father, love me despite my disobedience."

I had made a similar plea to my mother and father the first time I married Greg. The words then had been, "I know I'm greatly disappointing you both, but please love me and learn to love Greg." In my heart I knew that my Father in heaven was disappointed, but I was not strong enough to stand against my need for love and acceptance from my family. My prayer continued.

"Father, I believe in You. I believe in Your Word, the Bible. And I know the Christ of the New Testament, not the Christ the Mormons teach. And I will keep believing in You, but I want a life with my family. Please love me, Lord."

As we entered the parking lot, Greg's silent prayers became audible. "Somehow, Lord, turn this away. Help me to be strong enough not to go through with this. If it happens, correct us and help us deal with our error. Please send Your angels to watch over us and keep us. Thank You, dear Lord."

Greg had prayed aloud his own words and jumbled thoughts while I had been praying silently. But I couldn't respond to what he said. The battle that had been raging within me was now over, and my will was the temporary victor.

By 6:00 P.M. it was finished. Greg and Jolene Coe had been baptized into the Mormon Church. Now we drove home in a humiliating silence. In minutes the house would be filled with family and friends who wanted to celebrate this event with us.

As Greg and I entered the house, its empty silence was reminiscent of a mausoleum. All our possessions were there as we expected, but it felt vacant. This seemed like our first quiet moment since attending my sister's sacrament meeting.

With that silence came a horrifying realization. I felt Greg's eyes on me, and I turned to him and whispered, "What have we done?"

As if in response to my question, the heavens opened and a sharp clap of thunder crashed through the skies. Heavy drops of rain began to fall, ending in the most violent thunderstorm Tempe had received in years.

"It's as though the Lord is crying over the grave sin we've committed, Jolene." And with that we just stood staring at each other, almost afraid to move.

Three days after our baptism, Greg and I attended our first Gospel Doctrine Class at Sunday school. The teacher began the lesson by explaining that Jesus had exalted Himself to godhood by living a worthy and good life on earth. The teacher also explained that His father before Him, Elohim, had achieved his godhood in the same way.

Greg and I traded glances after that statement, knowing that this had no biblical support. Raising my hand, I asked the teacher where he had found this information since I was sure that it couldn't be in any of the 66 books of the Bible. In a condescending voice he assured me that as new converts we would come to realize the truth of what he was teaching if only we would sit quietly and listen carefully. At that I felt belittled and embarrassed in front of the others in the class. But this was typical of the answers given to the questions of the students.

During our first class, Greg and I saw a ray of light penetrate our darkness. But at this point we were not yet willing to confess our sins and forsake them, or, as the Scripture says, to be willing to hate mother and father and serve Jesus Christ (Luke 14:26). I could not say to my parents, "Jesus Christ means more to me than you do." Therefore I buried myself again in the Mormon Church. Greg and I devoured books on the history and doctrine of Mormonism, and attended all the church meetings and social events we possibly could. We even accepted jobs in the ward—Greg was to be the new Cub Scout committee chairman, and I was to serve as den mother.

Our involvement in the activities of the church came quickly and easy. There was no time to be "grounded in the faith," in the Mormon doctrine, before we were put to work in the church. No time was given us to prove ourselves worthy candidates for baptism, and there was no time to be discipled before taking certain leadership positions. To the members, we were trophies because once we had been anti-Mormon spokesmen, even appearing in an anti-Mormon movie, and had recently converted back to Mormonism. Consequently we were presented with the idea of promoting the LDS Church, of being key figures in a great movement of Mormon evangelism.

It wasn't long before a well-known newspaper of the LDS Church requested an interview for a feature article. The story of our conversion was printed, with pictures of our family. Then members of the church began to use this article as a means of discrediting the movie The God Makers.

Because these events were happening without our permission, we felt used. Once again our lives seemed to be moving along a course over which we had no control. Events were happening that we didn't want to happen. Because our life had taken on a direction we had not intended, we became more sensitive to wanting to do the Lord's will, not ours. And the Lord was faithful in His response to us. We became painfully aware of our sinfulness. Guilt about what we had done permeated our thoughts day and night. It surrounded our daily activities and crept into our dreams. We could not escape the fact that we had done something terribly wrong.

One August morning, five weeks after our baptisms, I received a phone call from a former Mormon. He requested to meet with Greg and me to know why we had joined the LDS Church after having been Christians. He wanted to understand the reasons behind our decision to be baptized as members of the Mormon Church. I invited him to come to our home the following evening.

When he arrived the next evening with Bible in hand, he introduced himself as George Rasmussen. As we sat down in the family room, he placed his Bible on his lap. With that, he proceeded to tell how he and his wife had been raised in a Mormon home and had faithfully attended the LDS Church. He explained that as he was studying the Mormon Scriptures, he stumbled onto contradictions and inconsistencies of Mormon doctrine that threatened his belief. While trying to find answers to the questions, George concluded that the Mormon Church did not have answers for his obvious and sincere questions. As George and his wife continued their search, they found their answers on the pages of the Bible. With their answers met, they accepted Jesus Christ as their Savior.

George had been a Christian for several years when we met, but nonetheless he was puzzled and disturbed about our recent conversion. What had changed our minds? he wondered. Had we found something he had overlooked? Had we found proof that he and his wife had missed? His questions to us were honest, but he doubted that we had found conclusive evidence that supported the claims of the Church of Jesus Christ of Latter-day Saints.

Greg and I were defenseless. We had no answers for

George. This acknowledgment brought into sharp focus the issue that Greg and I had tried to avoid. We were confronted by the horrible sin we had committed against God. We admitted that we had willfully sinned, allowing ourselves to be drawn away from Him by our own desires and by the influence of people.

Pain pierced my heart. I looked at Greg and saw him struggling inside with the same plea as he groped for a way to ask George to leave. Greg managed to tell him that we would call him to continue our discussion and thanked him for his concern. When the door closed behind George, we were left alone, bewildered by the recent events and empty.

For five weeks in the LDS Church, Greg and I had tried to avoid the painful admission that we had denied God. We had tried to let peace in my family replace the peace which only God can give. We had substituted the busy schedule of Mormon Church activities for the fullness of life which can only be found in Christ.

That night we knelt before God with contrite hearts, confessing our sin and asking for forgiveness. And the Lord answered our prayer and lifted the veil of darkness from our eyes.

Our five weeks of membership in the Mormon Church was a period of being blind to our faults, to falsehood, and to deception. Greg and I were Christians who were so familiar with the doctrine and lifestyle of the Church of Jesus Christ of Latter-day Saints that we should never have been tempted by it. Yet our desire for a sense of belonging and fellowship, and the emotional security found in my family, drew us into it.

We were Christians who knew better than to accept the Mormon way, yet we were blinded. The intense desire for peace with my family, for the acceptance of friends, and for friends who might not reject or disappoint us somehow kept us blind to the significance of what we were doing.

God used George to open our eyes. George had heard my story and had remembered it because of its similarity to his own. He too had left his Mormon family behind when he turned to Jesus. He too had struggled with the same sense of loss. He too had felt the pull away from Jesus, and the pull to return to his family and Mormon lifestyle.

Now a complete renunciation of the Mormon Church was necessary. We needed to renounce their doctrine and remove ourselves from the activities of the church. And we needed to once again reunite with a Christian church that was faithful to the Word of God and to surround ourselves with faithful Christians friends. Now we were ready to move forward together, "being confident of this very thing, that he which hath begun a good work in you will perform it until the day of Jesus Christ" (Philippians 1:6).

— Chapter 19 —

Not My Will

Cause me to hear thy lovingkindness in the morning, for in thee do I trust; cause me to know the way wherein I should walk, for I lift up my soul unto thee.

Psalm 143:8

My sadness was mixed with anger. Possibly Greg and I had been deceived by Satan and pressured by people, but we had been victimized by our own self-deception. We had to take responsibility for being lured into the Church of Jesus Christ of Latter-day Saints.

The apostle James says, "But every man is tempted when he is drawn away of his own lust and enticed. Then when lust has conceived, it bringeth forth sin: and sin, when it is finished, bringeth forth death" (James 1:14,15). Our temptation sprang from our own desire to be united with my family.

Once we confessed our weakness and responsibility, our relationship with the Lord Jesus Christ was restored. We gave Him our bodies, our family, our relationships—

everything that we are according to Romans 12:1,2.

We had joined the Mormon Church hoping that it would fill the void left by family and friends who had rejected us. We hadn't joined because of doctrinal beliefs or theological reasons. But there was little solace in this fact.

There were expressions of disappointment in us by friends, but there was little opportunity to answer them. Overconfident that their churches are far from the Mormon Church or other cults in religious lifestyle, they have little idea of the similar qualities and similar satisfaction. The prime difference is in doctrine.

We needed time to strengthen our relationship with God, with our family, and with our Christian friends. We wanted Proverbs 3:5,6 to become our guide: "Trust in the Lord with all thine heart, and lean not unto thine own understanding. In all thy ways acknowledge him, and he shall direct thy paths."

So we turned to God for forgiveness, comfort, and healing. We asked Him to make this a time of restoration rather than a time to nurture feelings of bitterness, guilt, and anger. We didn't want to return hurt for hurt. We asked Him to make us people after His will.

During this period of recovery, I was spending much time in prayer, not only for myself and my family, but for other people as well. One of my prayers was that God would reconcile us to my family and another was that we would be reconciled to Russ and Cindy. Thanks to God, the lines of communication are opening with my family. And as for Russ and Cindy, I can testify our friendship has been restored.

He also gave us courage to ask forgiveness from people we had hurt. Karen was a friend who seemed devastated by our mistake. Between sobs she choked out two words: "What happened?" The tightness in her voice spoke of her sorrow for us.

Greg and I couldn't explain to Karen or to anyone else

exactly what had happened. We knew that we had sinned when we joined the Mormon Church, and we knew that our witness for Jesus had been ruined for a time. Admitting this was extremely hard to do. At times we wanted to run away and hide from our sins.

Although the Bible is full of many examples of God's forgiveness, the greatest example is that of Jesus Christ's death on the cross. Jesus was the spotless, worthy Lamb sacrificed for the sins of every person. He suffered the incredible pain of crucifixion in order that we might enjoy fellowship with God and eternal life with Christ. While He hung on that cross, He bore the sins of everyone. He died for every one of us, without exception. Those of us who accept His death and acknowledge His resurrection and His lordship will be welcomed into heaven, but not everyone makes this choice.

The apostle Paul talks about people who do not choose to accept Christ: "Professing themselves to be wise, they became fools" (Romans 1:22). Greg and I had become such fools. We had not accepted all that the Mormon Church taught, but we had sat among them and listened as they exchanged the truth for a lie.

God showed favor toward us that we could never have earned, and accepted us back into His fold. And we acted on His promise: "If we confess our sins, he is faithful and just to forgive us our sins, and to cleanse us from all unrighteousness" (1 John 1:9).

As a member of the LDS Church, I believed that I must always be working to earn acceptance, whether that of God, my family, or my friends. This acceptance was earned on the treadmill of church activities that couldn't be slowed. If I kept pace, I would eventually have the title "worthy Latter-day Saint." My acceptance by other Mormons would be guaranteed.

As a Christian, however, I didn't need to work for God's acceptance. I didn't need to earn the title of "worthy" or "deserving." Because Christ is worthy, my sins are forgiven and I am accepted by Him. God is always willing and waiting to receive us. He knocks at the door of our hearts so that we will let Him enter. We have the choice of accepting or rejecting Him.

God was faithful to us while we were yet sinners. For a time we were wandering from Him like the children of Israel in the wilderness. But through it all, a maturation and stability has resulted in both Greg and me. We are now established in a church to worship and serve the Lord. Through our church and public ministry, many wonderful Christian friends have come into our lives. We are encouraged by them and by the progress we see in every member of our family.

Today Greg and I are testifying that Christ has died, Christ is risen, and Christ will come again. That is the gospel, and it demonstrates that we have been accepted by the mercy of God. That is the message we want to share with whoever comes to the door of our home or shares in our public ministry.

Daily we continue in prayer, in studying the Word, and in examination of ourselves. The seeds of heresy are in all of us, and they flourish where we are weak. We have experienced them, and their fruit is bitter. We want to be always vigilant to any manipulation or self-deception about denying Jesus Christ. Our desire is to "abide in him, that, when he shall appear, we may have confidence, and not be ashamed before him at his coming" (1 John 2:28).

— *Appendix* —

Investigations And
An Invitation

"The Church is definitely and fully Christian in every possible interpretation of that characterization," states Mormon President Stephen L. Richards of the First Presidency under the prophet David O. McKay. Other Latter-day Saints are also convinced that Mormonism is a completion of Christianity.

Let us compare eight basic doctrines of The Church of Jesus Christ of Latter-day Saints, found in their Scriptures, with the doctrines of Christianity, based on the Bible.

1. *MORMONISM: A History of the Church*

The Church of Jesus Christ of Latter-day Saints (Mormons) was founded by Joseph Smith in 1820. He claimed that he was the recipient of a marvelous vision. While he prayed in the woods near Palmyra, New York, he was privileged to have God the Father and God the Son appear and speak to him. The Mormon Church claims that "the Almighty restored His church to earth again." Joseph Smith believed that all churches were apostate and that he was called in this vision to "restore the gospel" (*Pearl Of Great Price*, Joseph Smith 2:1-25).

Mormonism teaches that Joseph Smith was a prophet, and that the true church must have a living prophet as a sign of its authenticity: "Joseph Smith, the Prophet and Seer of the Lord, has done more, save Jesus only, for the salvation of men in this world, than any other man that ever lived in it" (*Doctrine and Covenants* 135:3).

THE CHALLENGE

Restoration implies that something was lost, but the gospel of Christ was never lost. Followers of Christ have always had the mandate to proclaim, not to restore: "Go ye therefore and teach all nations, baptizing them in the name of the Father, and of the Son, and of the Holy Ghost, teaching them to observe all things whatsoever I have commanded you, and, lo, I am with you always, even unto the end of the world" (Matthew 28:19,20).

What is the gospel of Christ? The gospel message of the Bible is that Jesus Christ died for our sins, that He was buried, and that He was raised on the third day (1 Corinthians 15:1,3,4). This sacrificial act is the foundation of our salvation. By Christ's death and resurrection we are forgiven of our sins and are able to enjoy fellowship with God as we look forward to an eternity with Jesus. We are saved from our sinfulness and our guilt when we have faith in Jesus Christ. The truth of God is not embodied in a religious system but in the divine Person of the Lord Jesus Christ.

Does Joseph Smith meet the biblical requirements for a prophet of God? "When a prophet speaketh in the name of the Lord, if the thing follow not nor come to pass, that is the thing which the Lord hath not spoken, but the prophet hath spoken it presumptuously; thou shalt not be afraid of him" (Deuteronomy 18:22). In this critical point Joseph Smith failed. Many of his prophecies have proven false. An example is his prophecy of the Lord's return. In 1835 Joseph Smith prophesied that the coming of Jesus Christ was near, and that within 56 years this world would end (*The History of the Church*, Vol. 2, p. 182; Vol. 5, p. 336; Vol 1, p. 323; Vol. 2, p. 188).

Are Joseph Smith's prophecies in agreement with the prophecies of the Bible? To accept Joseph Smith as a prophet is to do so based only on his word and the testimony of his followers, but not in accordance with the Bible. A true prophet must be in agreement with all previous revelations (Deuteronomy 13:1-5). It is the duty of God's people to examine the prophecy against all previous prophecies: "But though we or an angel from heaven preach any other gospel unto you than that which we have preached unto you, let him be accursed" (Galatians 1:8).

2. MORMONISM: The Writings of the Church

The Church of Jesus Christ of Latter-day Saints has four authoritative books:

The *Book of Mormon* is allegedly the sacred history of the ancestors of the American Indians. Mormons claim that God spoke to American prophets just as He did to Hebrew prophets. These American Scriptures were recorded on gold plates which were given to Joseph Smith in 1827 and have since disappeared. Joseph Smith claimed to have translated the "Reformed Egyptian" writings into English by the "gift and power of God."

The *Doctrine and Covenants* is a collection of allegedly divine revelations and inspired declarations given for the establishment and regulation of the kingdom of God on earth in these last days.

The *Pearl of Great Price* is a selection of materials which addresses many significant aspects of the faith and doctrines of the Mormon Church. These writings were supposedly produced by the prophet Joseph Smith and published in the church periodicals of his day. According to the book's own introduction (paragraph 3), "Several revisions have been made in the contents as the needs of the church have required."

The Bible holds a less important place for Mormons among the four books. They believe that the Bible has been corrupted by translation errors and that there is need for a present-day revelation. In the Eighth Article of Faith, Joseph Smith said, "We believe the Bible to be the Word of God as far as it is translated correctly; we also believe the *Book of Mormon* to be the Word of God."

"As far as it is translated correctly" allows freedom for personal interpretation of the Bible, a freedom that ignores established principles and laws that govern the interpretation of any book. The Ninth Article of Faith increases this freedom: "We believe all that God has revealed, all that He does now reveal, and we believe that He will yet reveal many great and important things pertaining to the Kingdom of God." This statement is a disclaimer that allows for changes in doctrine when the doctrine is proven false or becomes difficult to live with.

Compare two prophecies of Joseph Smith with Bible passages: Joseph Smith said, "I saw two personages, whose brightness and glory defy all description, standing above me in the air. One of them spake unto me, calling me by name and said, pointing to the other—this is my Beloved Son. Hear Him!" (*Pearl of Great Price*, History 1:17).

The Bible says, "No man hath seen God at any time; the only begotten Son, which is in the bosom of the Father, he hath declared him" (John 1:18). God also said, "There shall no man see me and live" (Exodus 33:20).

Consider whether Joseph Smith's claim that we need a prophet for today is in agreement with the Bible: "God, who at sundry times and in diverse manners spake in time past unto the fathers by the prophets, hath in these last days spoken unto us by his Son, whom he hath appointed heir of all things, by whom also he made the worlds" (Hebrews 1:1,2). The Bible clearly states that prophecy has ceased. God's divine Word is complete. There is no more need for a prophet since God spoke to us through His Son, Jesus Christ.

THE CHALLENGE

The New Testament writers testify that the gospel of Christ is both complete and trustworthy. It will not change.

The apostle Paul writes, "I have fully preached the gospel of Christ" (Romans 15:19). The apostle Peter writes concerning God, "His divine power hath given unto us all things that pertain unto life and godliness" (2 Peter 1:3). The Bible testifies concerning itself that Scripture is complete. There is no need for more Scriptures.

Contradictions and confusion within Mormon Scriptures cast further doubt on the authenticity of the writings. Since it was printed, the *Book of Mormon* has undergone several thousand revisions! Consider these contradictions: "For do we not read that God is the same yesterday, today, and forever, and in Him there is no variableness neither shadow of changing" (Mormon 9:9, see also *Doctrine and Covenants* 20:17-19). This is contradicted by the *Teachings of the Prophet Joseph Smith* compiled by Joseph Fielding Smith, p. 345 and *The Journal of Discourses*, Vol. VI, p. 3: "God himself was once as we are now, and is an exalted man."

Mormon Church leaders also contradict Scripture. Joseph Smith taught and practiced polygamy because of a divine revelation he claims to have received. Yet the church's *Book of Jacob* forbids polygamy (Book of Jacob 2:24-28).

The *Book of Mormon* contradicts the Bible. Alma 7:10 states that Jesus was born in Jerusalem. The Bible states that Jesus was born in Bethlehem (Luke 2:4-7).

3. *MORMONISM: Man, Godhood, and the Heavenly Kingdoms*

Mormonism teaches: "As man is, God once was; as God is, man may become" (Lorenzo Snow). "You must learn how to be a God yourself, the same as all other Gods have done before you," states Brigham Young (*Journal of Discourses*, Vol. VI). There are many gods and these gods are polygamous, writes Milton R. Hunter (*The Gospel Through the Ages*) and Orson Pratt (*The Seer*).

Mormon prophets have continually taught that God, the eternal Father, was once a mortal man who passed through a school of earth life similar to the one each of us is passing through now. His obedience to the same eternal gospel truths which the Mormon Church advances today earned Him His godhood (*The Gospel Through the Ages*, Hunter, p. 104). The Mormon's *Doctrine and Covenants* (132:20,37) further explains this doctrine: "Then [after obedience to the Mormon instruction for life] shall they be gods, because they have all power, and the angels are subject unto them" and ". . . because they did none other things than that which they were commanded, they have entered into their exaltation, according to the promises and sit upon thrones, and are not angels but are gods." The doctrine that men can become gods and enjoy their godhood in one of the three heavenly kingdoms is fundamental to the lifestyle which the Mormon Church outlines for its members. Godhood is attained only by righteous living, obedience to church instruction, marriage in the temple, and adherence to the practices of the church.

THE CHALLENGE

"As man is, God once was" contradicts Mormon

Scripture as well as the Bible. The *Doctrine and Covenants* (20:17-19) teach an infinite, eternal, unchangeable God. The *Pearl of Great Price* (Moses 1:3) quotes God as saying to Moses, "Behold, I am the Lord God Almighty, and Endless is my name; for I am without beginning of days or end of years." The *Book of Mormon* (Moroni 8:18) states, "I know that God is not a partial God, neither a changeable being; but He is unchangeable from all eternity to all eternity."

Mormon doctrine contradicts the teachings of the Bible. Never does the Bible suggest that God was once man or that man is to become a god (1 John 3:1-3). Hear what the Bible teaches: "God is not a man, that he should lie, neither the son of man, that he should repent" (Numbers 23:19). "I am God, and not man" (Hosea 11:9). God is not a created being (John 1:1-5). He is from everlasting to everlasting (Psalm 90:2). He is unchangeable and eternal (Deuteronomy 33:27; Psalm 41:13; Isaiah 40:28).

"Before me there was no God formed, neither shall there be after me" (Isaiah 43:10). "I am the first and the last, and besides me there is no God" (Isaiah 44:6). God declares that there are no other gods, for this earth or any other.

"Ye shall be as gods," declared Satan (Genesis 3:5). Satan himself worked to attain godhood: "I will be like the Most High" (Isaiah 14:14). God answered with this vow: "Thou shalt be brought down to hell" (Isaiah 14:15). This declaration of the infinite God condemns the Mormon plan of men attaining godhood. As with Satan, this plan will lead to eternal damnation.

4. *MORMONISM: God—Flesh-and-Bones or Spirit?*

"The Father has a body of flesh and bones as tangible as man's; the Son also; but the Holy Ghost has not a body of flesh and bones, but is a personage of Spirit" (D&C 130:22). Prophet Joseph Smith claimed that he saw God in flesh and bones at the time of his vision.

THE CHALLENGE

Mormons believe that Jesus was "the express image" of the Father (Hebrews 1:3) and reason that the Father must also have a body of flesh and bones. Mormons then turn to Luke 24:39, where Jesus appears to His disciples: "Behold my hands and feet, that it is I myself; handle me and see, for a spirit hath not flesh and bones, as ye see me have." Earlier in that same chapter, though, Jesus taught two men who were traveling to Emmaus. When He finished talking with them and they realized who He was, Jesus "vanished out of their sight" (Luke 24:31). The Mormons bypass this verse, which indicates the difference between Jesus' body and man's body. They let verse 39 stand alone, and they let it stand as evidence of Jesus' fleshly body.

Mormons also look to the Old Testament Scriptures to prove that God has a flesh-and-blood body. They use metaphorical personifications as arguments for their view: The expression the "hand of the Lord" is one phrase that supports their claim. Carrying this approach one step further can lead to the ridiculous conclusion that God is a bird: David cries to be sheltered in "the shadow of thy wings" (Psalm 57:1). This obviously violates standard literary rules of interpretation.

Just as God is not a bird, neither does He have flesh and bones. The Bible states that "God is a spirit, and they that worship him must worship him in spirit and in truth" (John 4:24). Consider, too, that God is omnipotent (Genesis 17:1; Exodus 6:3), omnipresent (Psalm 139:7; Jeremiah 23:23), and omniscient (Psalm 139:1-6; Proverbs 5:21). These attributes are impossible for a flesh-and-blood being.

Consider the Mormon view of man's body. Genesis 1:26,27 states, "Let us make man in our image.... So

God created man in his own image." The truth of this passage is not that man is like God in a physical or fleshly likeness; man is instead created in a *spiritual likeness* to God.

In the New Testament, Colossians 3:10 explains the new life in Christ when we "have put on the new man, which is renewed in knowledge after the image of him that created him." When a person accepts the gospel of Jesus Christ, he does not change physically. The change that occurs is the renewing of the spiritual image of God. The change in the person is internal and spiritual (2 Corinthians 5:17). It is also worth noting that when the writer of Hebrews 1:3 describes Christ as the "express image" of God, he uses a Greek word that refers to the *inner* being, not the *physical* being. The Mormon Church, therefore, cannot legitimatcly use "man in God's image" as evidence that God has the same flesh-and-bone body that man does. The apostle Paul warns against making God in thc image of corruptible man (Romans 1:21-25).

5. *MORMONISM: Preexistence and Eternal Progression*

The Mormon doctrine of salvation is connected to their doctrine of a preexistent state of man. This begins with the idea that humans are as eternal as God is. The church then teaches four stages of mankind:

1. We are eternally existing "intelligences."
2. We are conceived by God with one of His wives, and we are born as a "premortal spirit."
3. We are born into the mortal probation of this earth, where we gain bodies of flesh and bone.
4. After life on this earth, we go to one of three heavenly kingdoms. The destination is determined by works performed during this life:

> The Telestial Kingdom is for those the Bible would condemn to hell. (See D&C 76:81-82.)

The Terrestrial Kingdom is for those who are good and righteous Mormons. (See D&C 76:71-79.)

The Celestial Kingdom is reserved for those baptized into the Church of Jesus Christ of Latter-day Saints, who live according to all of the church's laws and its gospel ordinances, and who are sealed in one of the Mormon temples. (See D&C 76:69-109.)

THE CHALLENGE

Many contradictions exist between the words of different Mormon leaders. Consider these three statements, the first being Joseph Smith's statement of the doctrine of man's eternal nature:

> I tell you, life did not commence upon this earth spontaneously. Its origin was not here.... There never was a beginning, never was a time when man did not exist somewhere in the universe, and when the time came for this earth to be peopled, the Lord our God, transplanted upon it from some other earth, the life which is found here (*Doctrines of Salvation*, Vol. I, pp. 139-40).
>
> When you tell me that father Adam was made as we make adobes from the earth, you tell me what I deem an idle tale.... There is no such thing in all the eternities where the Gods dwell. Mankind are here because they are offspring of parents who were first brought here from another planet (Brigham Young, *Journal of Discourses*, Vol. VII, pp. 285-86).
>
> Contrary to the belief of many, Adam did not receive his body in another world, but was clothed with a body of flesh and bones from the elements of this earth.... The scriptures teach that Christ is the only begotten of God in the flesh.... Therefore, since Adam was the son of God, not of mortals, and

was not literally begotten of God in the flesh, God created him of the dust of this earth as proclaimed in Genesis and Alma (Joseph Fielding Smith, the tenth president of the Mormon Church, *Doctrinal Answers*, pp. 103-04).

These three passages are inconsistent with each other. Furthermore, they all deny the truth of the Bible. Genesis 1 teaches that God created all things out of nothing. (See also John 1:1-5; Acts 17:24-26; Colossians 1:16). Genesis 2:7 gives some detail: "The Lord God formed man of the dust of the ground, and breathed into his nostrils the breath of life; and man became a living soul." The Bible, does not teach the Mormon doctrine of preexistence.

Only Jesus preexisted before coming to earth: "I am the living bread which came down from heaven" (John 6:51). He taught that no one else has come down from heaven: "No man hath ascended up to heaven but he that came down from heaven, even the Son of man which is in heaven" (John 3:13). Jesus' preexistence is evidence of His deity; it is not a precedent for our preexistence.

The Mormon doctrine of man's existence covers time after this life as well as time before this life. The time after this life will be spent in one of three heavenly kingdoms—the Telestial, the Terrestrial, or the Celestial. The Bible teaches only a heaven and a hell.

Mormon leaders use 1 Corinthians 15:40,41 as evidence for the existence of both a celestial and a terrestrial heaven. Paul's discussion of the glory of the sun (celestial) and the glory of the moon (terrestrial) is actually an answer to the earlier verse 35. The people of the Corinthian church had questions about the resurrection body they would one day receive. Look at the entire passage and see that Paul is illustrating the contrast between the mortal, corruptible body and the immortal, incorruptible body of the resurrection. The apostle is talking about *bodies*, not heavens.

Nevertheless, Mormons use this Corinthian verse to argue for three different heavens. They interpret verses 40 and 41 as references to celestial and terrestrial heavens. They have created a new word for the third heaven—which the Bible does not mention. This new word is "telestial," Joseph Smith's combination of the other two words. One other comment about the vocabulary the Mormons use: The word "terrestrial" refers to things of this earth. The phrase "Terrestrial Kingdom" or "Terrestrial Heaven" is a contradiction in terms.

The Mormon Church also relies on 2 Corinthians 12:2-4 to support their concept of three heavens where Paul refers to a third heaven. Again, this phrase needs to be interpreted in the biblical context. The Bible does teach three heavens. The first is what we could call the atmosphere (Genesis 7:23; Matthew 24:30). This is the domain of clouds, birds, and rain. The second heaven is "planetary," where the sun, moon, and stars exist (Genesis 1:14,15,17; 22:17; Psalm 19:1; Mark 13:25). The third heaven is the spiritual heaven that Paul refers to, and is the place where God and His angels dwell. Those who have found salvation in Jesus Christ will spend eternity there (Matthew 6:9; Mark 12:25; Philippians 3:20).

Mormonism preaches a general salvation for all people. The Bible repeatedly refutes this idea. The Bible teaches that there is one heaven and one hell (Matthew 7:21-23; Revelation 20:11-15) and that a person's destiny is his own choice: "Enter in at the strait gate; for wide is the gate and broad is the way that leadeth to destruction, and many there be which go in thereat; because strait is the gate and narrow is the way which leadeth unto life, and few there be that find it" (Matthew 7:13,14).

6. MORMONISM: Salvation, Power, and Authority

Without the atonement, the gospel, the priesthood,

and the sealing power, there would be no salvation. Without continuous revelation...there would be no salvation. If it had not been for Joseph Smith and the restoration, there would be no salvation. There is no salvation outside The Church of Jesus Christ of Latter-day Saints (*Mormon Doctrine*, pp. 669-70).

We believe that a man must be called of God by prophecy, and by the laying on of hands, by those who are in authority to preach the gospel and administer in the ordinances thereof (The Fifth Article of Faith, by Joseph Smith).

Mormon priesthood has divine authority to act for God; that men holding this priesthood possess part of God's power and are in reality part of God; that to reject this authority is to reject God (*The Gospel Through the Ages*, by Hunter; *Articles of Faith*, by Talmadge; and *A New Witness for God*, by B. H. Roberts).

THE CHALLENGE

The Mormon Church is structured by a priesthood of two orders, the Melchizedek order (the higher) and the Aaronic (the lesser) (D&C 107:1). The Mormon handbook *A Uniform System for Teaching Investigators* (1971 edition, pp. 14-15) explains the origin of the priesthood: "Yes, he [Jesus] gave them [the apostles] the power or authority to act in his name. This authority of the scriptures is called the PRIESTHOOD." This justification of the Mormon priesthood, however, has no biblical support. Nowhere does it say in the Bible that Jesus delegated a "priesthood" on the apostles; nowhere did Jesus teach that a person must be a "priest" in order to "act for God."

The Mormon Church teaches that without this priesthood all of its ordinances (baptism, sacraments, blessings, healings, temple endowments, temple marriages, baptism for the dead, etc.) would be invalid. They teach that they are the only true church on the earth because of the power and authority of the priesthood. They believe that no other person, group of people, or church can "act for God."

In the Old Testament there was only one legal high priest at any given time. Once a year this priest would offer up a blood sacrifice for himself and for the people. During the period of the New Testament and since, Jesus Christ became the one and only Mediator or High Priest between God and man (1 Timothy 2:5). And Jesus Christ is the sacrifice for our sins at the same time that He is our High Priest. This twofold role is eternal in its significance: "This man, because he continueth ever, hath an unchangeable priesthood" (Hebrews 7:24). Furthermore, Jesus offered His body as the perfect sacrifice for our sins. No longer does man have to offer sacrifices for his sin. That sacrifice was completed in Christ Jesus, and there is no need for a priesthood on earth today (Hebrews 3:1; 7:9-12,26,27; 8:1-6; 9:11,12,25,26; 10:10-14; for an in-depth study, see *Mormon Claims Answered*, by Marvin W. Cowan).

While there is no formal priesthood on earth today and no need for one, Christians are members of a "holy" and "royal" priesthood (1 Peter 2:5,9). Jesus did not bestow any special authority on a certain order of people. Instead, He provided all Christians with the Holy Spirit. The Spirit dwells within each believer, and, as Jesus promised, "he will guide you into all truth" (John 16:7-15). God's Son has taught us how to live and has provided us a Comforter and a Teacher in the Holy Spirit. An earthly priesthood is not necessary.

7. *MORMONISM: The Temple and Its Purpose*

Temples are built for the performance of sacred ordinances—not secret, but sacred.... After a

Temple is dedicated only members of the church in good standing may enter.... One of the distinguishing features of the restored Church of Jesus Christ is the eternal nature of its ordinances and ceremonies.... In the house of the Lord [temple]...the marriage ceremony is performed by those who are properly authorized...[and] the union between husband and wife, and between parents and children, is effected for time and all eternity (*The Purpose of the Temple*, by David O. McKay).

Temples have a major role in the religious system of the Mormon Church. Besides being the site of the sealing of husband and wife and of parents and children, the temple is also the place for baptism for the dead, temple endowments, and marriage by proxy for those married couples who died without a temple marriage which would have sealed them for time and all eternity. Genealogical research is also implemented at the temple, and it is the responsibility of every church member to provide salvation for the dead: "The greatest responsibility in this world that God has laid upon us is to seek after our dead.... Those Saints who neglect it in behalf of their deceased relatives, do it at the peril of their own salvation" (*Teachings of the Prophet Joseph Smith*, by Joseph Fielding Smith, pp. 193, 356).

THE CHALLENGE

In the Old Testament, temples were the site of sacrifice and worship. Never were they the place for marriage ceremonies or ceremonies for the dead. Nor were they needed for ceremonies "which pertain to salvation and exaltation in the Kingdom of God," a requirement in the Mormon Church (*Mormon Doctrine*, by McConkie, pp. 779-80). Later, the New Testament writers completely reject the idea of a temple for God made by man's hands.

In the book of Acts, Stephen and Paul both explain that the Lord "dwelleth not in temples made with hands" (Acts 7:48; 17:24). The writer of the epistle to the Hebrews, who thoroughly discusses the priesthood of Jesus Christ as the fulfillment of the Old Testament priesthood, also mentions the temple. He explains that "Christ is not entered into the holy places made with hands...but into heaven itself, now to appear in the presence of God for us" (Hebrews 9:24).

The temple which is most referred to by Jesus and by the New Testament writers is the physical body of each believer. Paul writes, "Know ye not that ye are the temple of God, and that the Spirit of God dwelleth in you?" (1 Corinthians 3:16). In 1 Corinthians 6:19,20 and 2 Corinthians 6:16, Paul never mentions a temple of stone.

The Bible not only offers a different view of the temple, but it also offers different ideas concerning the rituals that Mormons perform in their temple. Nowhere does the Bible teach that marriages are to be contracted for time and all eternity. Romans 7:2 is specific: "The woman which hath a husband is bound by law to her husband so long as he liveth." Marriage is an institution of this life only. Jesus Himself explained to the Sadducees that "in the resurrection they neither marry nor are given in marriage, but are as the angels of God in heaven" (Matthew 22:30). This verse not only refutes the Mormon concept of eternal marriage but contradicts their corollary teaching that residents of the Celestial Kingdom will procreate. Just as there is no marriage, there is no procreation.

The Mormons also practice baptism for the dead in their temples. This is based upon a misinterpretation of 1 Corinthians 15:29: "What shall they do which are baptized for the dead if the dead rise not at all? Why are they then baptized for the dead?" Here Paul is reassuring new Christians that their future resurrection is certain because of the previous resurrection of Christ. He is not teaching a doctrine of baptism for the dead.

While 1 Corinthians 15:29 may be a difficult passage, it certainly does not support an entire doctrine of baptism for the dead. If baptism for the dead were as important to salvation as Mormonism claims, then surely Jesus Himself would have taught us about it.

8. *MORMONISM: Salvation—General and Individual*

Salvation is twofold: General—that which comes to all men irrespective of a belief in Christ—and Individual—that which man merits through his own acts through life and by obedience to the laws and ordinances of the gospel (*Doctrines of Salvation*, by Joseph Fielding Smith, Vol. I, p. 134).

The first effect [of the atonement] is to secure to all mankind alike, exemption from the penalty of the fall, thus providing a plan of General Salvation. The second effect is to open a way for Individual Salvation whereby mankind may secure remission of personal sins. As these sins are the result of individual acts, it is just that forgiveness for them should be conditioned on individual compliance with prescribed requirements—obedience to the laws and ordinances of the Gospel (*Articles of Faith*, by James Talmage, p. 87).

There will be a General Salvation for all in the sense in which the term is generally used, but salvation, meaning resurrection, is not exaltation (*Contributions of Joseph Smith*, by Stephen L. Richards, p. 5).

All men are saved by grace alone without any act on their part, meaning they are resurrected (*What the Mormons Think of Christ*, by Bruce R. McConkie, p. 28).

THE CHALLENGE

The Mormon Church makes a distinction between general and individual salvation, and it equates general salvation with resurrection. Neither of these teachings is supported by the Bible.

First, the Bible does not teach a "general salvation." The Bible is specific in teaching that salvation comes only through faith in Jesus Christ. Salvation comes only to those people who receive the Lord Jesus Christ as their Savior. Many verses set forth this truth: "Believe on the Lord Jesus Christ, and thou shalt be saved" (Acts 16:31); "I am the way, the truth, and the life; no man cometh unto the Father but by me" (John 14:6); "As many as received him, to them gave he power to become the sons of God, even to them that believe on his name" (John 1:12). See also John 3:16,36; 5:24; Ephesians 2:8,9; Romans 6:23.

The Bible also teaches that every person who has ever lived upon this earth will be resurrected and judged in order to determine his eternal destiny (Revelation 20:11-15; Daniel 12:2; Matthew 25:46). Those people who believed in Jesus Christ while they lived on earth will receive eternal life with God in heaven. Those who rejected Jesus will be cast into hell for eternity (Revelation 20:10-15; 21:8). Each person will go the way of his decision, whether for or against Christ. At the time of the resurrection, however, "at the name of Jesus every knee should bow...and every tongue should confess that Jesus Christ is Lord" (Philippians 2:10,11). Even those people who once denied Christ will ultimately realize His lordship.

The Mormon Church, however, does not acknowledge the lordship of Jesus or the sufficiency of His death on the cross. According to Mormon doctrine, there are some sins which the blood of Jesus Christ cannot cover. Joseph Fielding Smith explains: "But man may commit certain grievous sins, according to his light and knowledge that will place him beyond the reach of the atoning blood of Christ. If then he would be saved he must make sacrifice of his own life to atone, so far as in his power lies, for that sin, for the blood of Christ alone under certain circumstances will not avail" (*Doctrines of Salvation*, pp. 133-34).

The Mormon Church points to sacrifice of self as a means of atoning for sins which Christ's death supposedly does not cover. Yet even this sacrifice will not be sufficient if the person has not been baptized into the Mormon Church; has not kept the commandments, laws, and ordinances of the Mormon Church; has not believed and confessed that all the prophets of the Mormon Church are prophets of God; and has not been married in an LDS temple.

The Bible has a very different message about personal salvation: "He that believeth on the Son hath everlasting life, and he that believeth not the Son shall not see life, but the wrath of God abideth on him" (John 3:36). The Scriptures make very clear the fact that each of us is a sinner (Romans 3:23) and that we can do nothing to save ourselves (Ephesians 2:8,9). God, because of His great love for mankind, provided us a way of salvation through Jesus Christ (2 Corinthians 5:21; John 3:16). Jesus shed his own blood on the cross for all people, for all sins, for all eternity (Hebrews 10:10,12,14-18). "Ye know that ye were not redeemed with corruptible things, as silver and gold...but with the precious blood of Christ, as of a lamb without blemish and without spot" (1 Peter 1:18,19). Salvation is a free gift from God (Romans 6:23). When we confess our sins and believe that Jesus died for our sins, we are saved (Acts 16:30,31; John 3:18; Romans 5:1; 3:24; 4:5).

Even without this gospel, the Mormon Church maintains that it is the only true church. The Bible, however, teaches that the one true church is not an organization.

Instead, it is the body of Christ, the body of believers, which He loved and purchased with His own blood (Ephesians 5:25; Colossians 1:24; Acts 20:28). Jesus stands at the head of the church and welcomes anyone who receives Him as Lord and Savior. Jesus said, "Him that cometh to me I will in no wise cast out" (John 6:37). Earthly organizations are important gatherings for worship, study, and support, but the spiritual unity with Christ as Head is the real church.

• • •

It should now be quite clear that the Mormon Church is not a Christian Church, that the Mormon God is not the God of the Bible, that the Mormon Jesus is not the Jesus of the Bible, and that the Mormon plan of salvation is not the biblical plan of salvation. Still, people commit their lives to the Mormon doctrine. Proverbs 14:12 cautions those people: "There is a way which seemeth right unto a man, but the end thereof are the ways of death." On the surface or from a distance, the Mormon Church may look like the right way. The Mormon people with their good works and moral lives can appear to be Christians. The heart of their faith, however, is hollow. They have substituted vain imaginings for the truth of Jesus Christ.

For much of my life I substituted the Mormon way of life for the true way of Jesus Christ (John 14:6). Now, however, Jesus Christ is the light of my world (John 8:12). He has revealed my false ways and has given me a real purpose and a real joy. Do you know the Lord Jesus Christ? Do you know His life-changing power? If you don't, here's how:

RECEIVE JESUS CHRIST: New life, a new beginning, and a new purpose can be yours when you receive Jesus as your Savior and your Lord (2 Corinthians 5:17-21). Faith in Him is the only criterion for your salvation (John 1:12,13; Acts 16:31). Once you believe, you will walk in the light of His truth (Ephesians 2:8-10).

THE RESULT? You will be guided and taught by the Holy Spirit (Romans 8:9-17). You will also experience the fruit of new life, and that fruit is changed attitudes and actions: "The fruit of the Spirit is love, joy, peace, longsuffering, gentleness, goodness, faith, meekness, temperance" (Galatians 5:22,23).

THE RESPONSIBILITY: The Bible warns believers not to be deceived by good works, good lives, or forms of godliness. The test of a person of God is that person's doctrine. Study God's Word. Become grounded in the teachings of Christ. Come to know the Holy Bible. Let your new life shine as a beacon of light in your corner of the world so that others might also be saved.

I pray that if you don't know Him, you will soon come to know Jesus Christ, "whom to know is life eternal."

"Receive the Word with all readiness of mind, and search the Scriptures daily, whether these things are so" (Acts 17:11).

"Prove all things; hold fast that which is good" (1 Thessalonians 5:21).